FINDING PERSONAL SIGNIFICANCE

The Old Testament Character of Jonah

By
Marc Royer Ph.D.

FINDING PERSONAL SIGNIFICANCE

The Old Testament Character of Jonah

Published by:
The Christian Resource Group
717 Bainbridge Place
Goshen, IN 46526
(574) 533-5133

ISBN: 0-9705958-7-5
Library of Congress Control Number: 2006905216

Printed in the United States by Morris Publishing
3212 East Highway 30
Kearney, NE 68847
1-800-650-7888

OTHER BOOKS BY DR. MARC ROYER

Secrets: Exposing, Resolving & Overcoming the Secrets We Carry with Us
Handling Death Dying and Grief
Rejection: Turning Your Lemons into Lemonade
Happiness in 30 Days or Less
Financial Freedom Starting Today
Practical Patience
The Development Manual Series
Volume I: A Study in the Old Testament
Volume II: A Study in the New Testament
A Study in the Life of David
A Study in the Prophets
Hell No!
Square Peg, Round Hole
Hocus Focus
The Spiritual Warfare Manual
Go Hard or Go Home
Removing the Obstacles to Effective Leadership Vol. 1
Instructions in Opposition Vol. 2
Soar: Effective Leadership Lessons Vol. 3
Dirty Words

Write:
The Christian Resource Group
717 Bainbridge Place
Goshen, IN 46526

Or visit our web site at www.tcrg.org
Request These Titles from Your Local Bookstore

Table of Contents

SIGNIFICANCE AS A CONCEPT

The #1 most important need in the life of the individual is the need to make a difference.

We can call this need—the need for significance—or—the need to be significant.

The need to be significant goes to the deepest part of our inner being. It can't be denied. It can't be excused. It can't be "grown out of." It has to be fulfilled.

Every person on the planet has a need for significance—and every one of them is trying to find a way to meet the need!

Whether you define it as "self esteem"—"self identity"—"insecurity"—or other self help/pop psychology diagnosis: FINDING PERSONAL SIGNIFICANCE is the key to its fulfillment.

Young people find a group (or a gang) with which to identify and belong. Adults find ways to gain personal significance through careers, education, or a softball league. Even the youngest child who is always putting up his/her hand to talk in class is trying to find personal significance.

Accepting the fact that each of us is attempting in our daily lives to find personal significance is the first step to fulfilling the need. Next, we need a template—some kind of a model to keep us on track. Who better for a guide than Jonah as recorded in the Bible's Old Testament? It is hard to tell if Jonah is a man who is mentally ill, a monster (evil incarnate), or our role model!

The Old Testament book titled by his name doesn't reveal a very large portion of his life. Actually, we see less than a month (and that might even be stretching it) of Jonah's entire life. In this short glimpse of Jonah's life, we experience in a vivid account, the depth of the human character in fear, reaction, submission, application, energy, and response that occurs in finding personal significance.

This study is designed as a starting point. Finding personal significance is a life long endeavor. Use as much of Jonah's story as you can apply—remember that the most important thing is the realization that we all are trying to find personal significance in our lives.

FINDING PERSONAL SIGNIFICANCE IS A LIFE LONG ENDEAVOR!

Chapter 1:"Everyone Has a Direction"
Jonah 1:1-2

[1]"Now the word of the LORD came to Jonah the son of Amittai, saying, [2]"Arise, go to Nineveh, that great city, and cry out against it; for their wickedness has come up before Me."

One of the first emotional fears people think of in regard to their life is—"I don't really have a direction." When a person feels a lack of direction he/she will normally experience a lack of significance.

BUT EVERYONE HAS A DIRECTION! It is placed inside them by God at birth.

EVERY PERSON WHO IS BORN IS DIRECTED NATURALLY TO:

1. Arise

2. Go to Nineveh

3. Cry out against it

Every Single Person Is Born with Direction In His or Her Life!

ARISE!

The first direction every single person who is born has is to "Arise!" "Arise" comes from the Hebrew word *(qum)* and has at least nine powerful applications to its meaning.

Each application can jump start the search in finding personal significance.

1. **Get Up.** Don't ever stay down—no matter what put you down, got you down, or turned you over. Get back up as fast as you possibly can. Sometimes people are down and don't realize it. There is not much you can do to "Arise" if you are down and can't see it—but—as soon as you do realize it—GET UP AS SOON AS POSSIBLE.

2. **Accomplishment.** Always be accomplishing something at any time in your life. The "What" of accomplishment is not important—the "Pursuit" of accomplishment is important! There is no accomplishment that is too small to be regarded as significant—especially in light of finding personal significance in your life. Any major accomplishment that exists in someone's life is a result of a series of smaller components to the major accomplishment or simply the sum of a series of small accomplishments. Either way, no accomplishment is ever too small!

3. **Confirm/Affirm.** Every person is born with the need to be affirmed emotionally, and hence,

be confirmed as a person. Affirmation is all part of finding personal significance. The concept that needs to be taught, (and it should be modeled in our upbringing, but rarely is any more), is the personal responsibility we all have to reach out to others and affirm them. The way a person is affirmed emotionally, (and confirmed as a person), is by reaching out and affirming and confirming others first, (without waiting for it to happen to me first.)

YOU CAN'T WAIT AROUND TO BE AFFIRMED BY OTHERS—YOU NEED TO REACH OUT AND BE THE ONE DOING THE AFFIRMING.

---

4. Performance. The word "performance" has a negative connotation in our culture. People connect the idea of "performance" with something being "fake." As far as direction in your life goes, this connection to

performance/fake is true, but only in a positive direction. Most of the time the best a person who is finding personal significance in his/her life can hope for, is the old idea that I "fake it until I make it." As rough as that phrase sounds, it actually means "I'm going to do my best and plow through it, learning as I go." Further, I'm not going to try to gain sympathy from others with my sob story. I'm going to do my best and learn from my mistakes. *The idea of performance is positive and powerful!*

"FAKE IT UNTIL YOU MAKE IT" ISN'T AS BAD AS IT SOUNDS!

---

5. Pitching In. We are born with the desire to pitch in and make a difference. Of course the desire needs to be "tweaked" a little here and there as we go, but for the most part, the natural component is for us to "arise"—to pitch in and make a difference. Leave the place better than you found it. Don't sit back on your hands. Get up and in to the game. Don't settle for "sitting it out" on the side lines.

6. **Remaining Steady.** We are born with the innate sense of direction to remain steady regardless of our circumstances. The reason this "built in sense" doesn't work is because we get in a big rush and don't let the natural course of life occur.

WE ARE ALL BORN WITH THE ABILITY TO REMAIN STEADY AND STABLE—AS LONG AS WE DON'T GET INTO A RUSH OVER THINGS.

---

7. **Strengthening Yourself as You Go.** Every one is able to grow stronger in the face of every circumstance. This ability to learn as you go comes naturally and should aid in finding personal significance. Learning as you go creates strength. The stronger you are, the less insecure you should be. The stronger you are the better esteem you should possess. The stronger you are, the greater the impact you can have in your life—hence—the greater the degree of significance. Learn as you go and you will learn as you grow!

11

> # Learn as you go and you will learn as you grow!

8. **Success.** Everyone is born with the potential for success. That does not mean there won't be such a thing as failure—it means you have the capacity to achieve success no matter what it is you face in your life. Every single person who is born—is born with the capacity to change every event they face into a successful situation. It is in this context that significance is synonymous with success—because any time you experience significance you experience success—even if it would appear like a failure to the rest of the world. Failure gives us just another opportunity to gain significance by turning things around. This direction for the potential of success is built within us from birth.

9. **Establishing.** Most people don't have enough confidence in themselves to see they are or can be an establisher. Yet, we are instilled with the direction to establish: to create, to dig a foundation, to build, and to grow.

   There is nothing in life more significant than establishing something. Why do so many people see the work of creating, building and growing as someone else's work or calling?

Because we are so busy trying to find personal significance that we forget to SIMPLY BE SIGNFICANT! Significance happens every single day of our lives—as we create, build, and grow our lives.

SIGNIFICANCE HAPPENS EVERY DAY OF OUR LIVES AS WE CREATE, BUILD, AND GROW. SIGNIFICANCE IS NOT SOMETHING YOU DO—IT IS WHO YOU ARE—ALL YOU HAVE TO DO IS BE SIGNIFICANT AND YOU WILL BE!

GO TO NINEVAH!

We are all born with the direction in our inner being to: "GO TO NINEVAH."

Ninevah was the capital of Assyria. In Jonah's time it was the center of everything.

- Anything that was anything was found in Ninevah.

- Anyone who was anyone could be found in Ninevah.

- Nothing existed that had any worth at all that wasn't somehow tied into Ninevah.

Ninevah was where the action was—and it means exactly the same thing here. We are all born with the direction to go and be where the action is.

We are not supposed to run away, hide, or excuse ourselves. Every single person is born with the natural ability to go towards the action—not away from it!

WE ARE BORN WITH THE NEED TO BE WHERE THE ACTION IS!

The word "GO" (halak) is a well known concept in the Bible but also has several important applications with regard to Ninevah.

Ninevah doesn't come to you—you must go to it!

"GO" IS A CONCEPT MEANING "CONTINUAL."
We are born with the direction to keep going at it—not to quit, run, or hide. We are equipped from birth with the inner drive to continue whatever we are doing—and in large part to pursue continually in our desire to be where the action is.

"GO" IS A CONCEPT MEANING COMMUNICATION.
We are born with the need and desire to communicate. Building relationship starts with relating to one another. Finding personal significance is based upon relating to others and building relationship.

"GO"
- **Continual**
- **Communication**
- **Leadership**
- **Adventure**

"GO" IS A CONCEPT MEANING TO BE A LEADER.

We are born with the ability to blaze our own path through life. Although the idea of leadership scares people, it is drive that is in-born.

If everyone was a leader, who would be left to lead? The sense of leadership is born within us—not necessarily the leadership of others—but the leadership of ourselves. Standing on your own two feet and making decisions is an important capacity for leadership from which many shy away. Yet—we are born with the natural direction to make our own decisions for ourselves and living with the result. Living life in this way means we have no one to blame but ourselves—developing the confidence for more decision making.

"GO" IS A CONCEPT MEANING TO SENSE THE ADVENTURE BEFORE YOU.

We are born with the interest in an adventure. Looking forward to each and every day is our natural drive in life. Enjoying each moment is a choice we all have—not to enjoy is more unnatural than it is natural.

IT IS NATURAL TO ENJOY YOUR LIFE FROM BIRTH—(UNNATURAL NOT TO ENJOY IT)!

CRY AGAINST IT!

The third part of our natural direction in life has to do with our approach toward things that matter (and things that don't). WE ARE TO BE PURPOSEFUL IN EVERYTHING WE DO!

The whole idea of cry (qara) is purposeful—literally meaning—"addressing someone properly and then accosting them."

"Against" literally means "UP AGAINST."

SO—"Cry against it"—means: BE PURPOSEFUL WHEN YOU GO UP AGAINST ANYTHING!

What does it mean to be purposeful going up against something?

- You are always moving forward. The motion of your life is forward—not backward—or looking back.

- You are always able to answer the "why" question concerning anything you do. Purposeful people know why they are doing what they are doing—about anything they are doing!

- You are able to move with "sure" steps. You don't second guess yourself.

Thoughts to Ponder

- Everyone is born with a definite direction in his/her life.

- Get up as soon as possible when you find yourself down.

- Instead of waiting to be affirmed, reach out to someone else and affirm them.

- We are born with the drive to pitch in and make a difference.

- Everyone is born with the desire to be where the action is.

- We might as well work at our communication since we all have a natural need to communicate.

- It is more natural to enjoy your life every single day rather than not to enjoy it.

- Always move forward.

- Make sure every step you take you take with sureness—because we are born with a sense of purpose in us.

Chapter 2: "When You Run—It Is Running from God" 1:3

³"But Jonah arose to flee to Tarshish from the presence of the LORD. He went down to Joppa, and found a ship going to Tarshish; so he paid the fare, and went down into it, to go with them to Tarshish from the presence of the LORD."

Running away from something is an attempt to find personal significance.

The need/drive to find personal significance is so strong in us that often we feel trapped, stressed, and drained. When a person feels this way the only recourse is to run away, quit, give up, or hide.

All of these reactions are always justified by the person who is running away—and often explained in such terms that it is hard to decipher that it really is running away, giving up, hiding, or quitting.

The reason people run is because they aren't finding the personal significance necessary to motivate them to stay—that is why running away must be broken down.

RUNNING AWAY IS AN ATTEMPT TO FIND PERSONAL SIGNIFICANCE.

Flee—Run—Hide:

Whatever it is you are going away from-- it is always from "the presence of the Lord."

Whenever you run away you are running from God's help for your life.

The truth is—no one can ever find personal significance apart from a relationship with God. Anything that resembles significance apart from God is just a fake—because only a relationship with God is the pursuit that gives a person true significance.

Whatever you think made you bolt from a situation may be different from what actually made you run away—it is this truth that has to be considered: The thing that actually made you run away is the need to find personal significance.

The thing that compels me to run away is the need for personal significance.

The truth is—what ever reason you give people for giving up or quitting—the REAL reason is that you have a deep need to find personal significance. You give up or quit because you aren't finding significance in what you are doing.

> # There is the reason you tell people you quit something—and then the REAL REASON you did.

If a person could come to grips with the fact that I want to run away, hide, quit, or give up because I am not finding personal significance in this situation—A PROFOUND SENSE OF PERSONAL AWARENESS WOULD RESULT!

Running away is usually a reactionary response to a certain event. It happens this way so we can blame our reaction on something and point to it. Often we are so focused on the "certain event" that we don't analyze the reaction—hence, we pretty much get by with it!

Getting by with something is not what is best for us at all—plus—we aren't able to find personal significance in "the next cool thing" that gets our attention and drags us along. Most of the time when we run from something, we think we are running to something else.

This isn't true at all—when you run from something you are running away from it.

> # When you run from something you aren't running toward something else—you are just running away!

In addition to the games you have played with your own mind—whatever you think it will be like away from the thing you are running away from—it will be miserable! You will be miserable, lonely, and confused because you have run away from the presence of the Lord.

When you feel trapped you need to take a few minutes and talk some sense into yourself.

Running away, quitting, or giving up should not be in the realm of options—finding personal significance is the only option—and that can only happen when you open up to the reality that significance can happen in the moment I am in—through the situation I am facing.

When you run—it is always "down."

"He went down to Joppa"

The geography is symbolic—and the symbolism is anything but trite. "Going down" has four powerful ramifications.

1. "Down" means letting loose of your potential in your current situation.

   Whenever you run away the potential in your current situation goes completely down the drain. There is no way to recover it—or take it with you to the next situation.

   You always have to start over when ever you "start over."

   It is only self-denial that makes you think you can transfer or rebuild the potential good in one situation when running away from one situation to go to another.

> You always have to start over when you "start over."

2. **"Down" means a degeneration of one's attitude toward a situation.**

There are many ways a person carries baggage with them when they run away. One of the ways they carry baggage is through their attitude.

Attitude problems are hard to hide because they come out in so many different ways. A person's attitude "oozes" from every pore in his/her body and mind.

When a person runs away from a situation there is always an attitude that follows with it. The attitude "baggage" feeds on itself, creating additional attitude and (baggage) problems to develop, grow, and fester.

Attitude problems ooze from every pore of a person's being—people who run away ooze their attitude!

---

3. "Down" means cutting out your aptitude for success.

   The more you run away the less likely you are to accomplish success in the next (new) situation. The reason for this is a person who runs away is less likely to even recognize success—and then, in turn, to acknowledge success.

4. "Down" means the losing of your grip on the destiny.

   When ever a person runs away he puts himself/herself in the hands of other people or situations. The likelihood of any situation or person bringing the person closer to finding personal significance is small.

People who run away are less likely to accomplish success because they are less likely to recognize or acknowledge success when it occurs.

The deception

You will always find a ship to take you wherever you want to go—deceiving you that running away is okay.

There are plenty of ships taking people in the opposite direction of where they are supposed to go.

Why would there be so many ways to run away if you aren't supposed to run away? Isn't that the deceiving part of it? Just because there is a ship to take you away doesn't mean you are supposed to go away!

> # WHY WOULD THERE BE SO MANY SHIPS GOING IN YOUR DIRECTION IF YOU AREN'T SUPPOSED TO RUN AWAY?

Just because you can find a way out doesn't mean you should get out.

Just because you can quit doesn't mean you should quit. Finding personal significance is contingent upon your own ability to resist running away just because you get the chance.

There is always a way out—don't ever think that since you found one that it is the indication you should. What you should always be looking for is personal significance—which is never found by going away—but by going into and toward!

There will always be people who will tell you to quit, run away, or to hide. Just because you have people who agree with you or think you should run away doesn't mean you should. You can always find someone who thinks running away is the thing to do.

YOU CAN ALWAYS FIND SOMEONE WHO WANTS YOU TO RUN AWAY OR QUIT—BUT ONLY BECAUSE IT MAKES THEM FEEL BETTER ABOUT THEMSELVES!

The reason people want you to run away is because it makes them feel better about themselves—the whole thing is selfish!

Don't fall into the affirmation of people who have run away themselves. Additionally—it might as well be said—most of the people on the ship you are on will be these people—All of them running away from the thing that will help them the most in finding personal significance.

Remember when you are on a ship taking you away from finding personal significance and the people around you are all affirming that you have done the right thing by running, quitting, or hiding that only one thing is true—THEY ARE ALL IN THE SAME "BOAT" AS YOU!

There is always a price

"So he paid the fare."

Ah yes....the price! The price for the fare when running away or quitting something you are supposed to stay with is always substantial.

The price is not something that can be measured with a dollar sign—it is far more costly than any amount of money. The price we pay for running away costs us dearly when it comes to our greatest need of all—the need to find significance. Because when we run away we run away (not toward) finding personal significance.

Part of the price (and this is a small part) is the exhaustion, self-doubt, and confusion running away brings.

The price for running away is outrageously expensive—it is the value of NOT BEING ABLE TO FIND YOUR PERSONAL SIGNIFICANCE.

Whenever you leave the presence of the Lord you will always get sucked or pulled in

"And went down into it, to go with them to Tarshish from the presence of the Lord."

A person who runs away is running from the presence of God. This is a person who has lost his/her ability to stand strong and steady. He/she is a person who is likely to fall for anything.

The person who runs away—who is running from finding personal significance—is likely to get pulled into all kinds of things that aren't beneficial.

> **A person who runs away is likely to get pulled or sucked into any thing.**

<u>Thoughts to Ponder</u>

- Running away is an attempt in finding personal significance.

- When you run away you are running from God's help in your life.

- When you run away you are always going in a downward or degenerative direction.

- You will always find a ship going the way you want to go—don't take that as a sign you should be running away.

- You will always find people to agree with what you are doing—keep in mind they are all on the same ship with you—likely running away too.

- Don't fool yourself—there is always a price to pay for running away.

- A person who is running away is easily pulled or sucked into anything.

Chapter 3: "Learn How to Float for Extended Periods of Time" 1:4

[4]"But the LORD sent out a great wind on the sea, and there was a mighty tempest on the sea, so that the ship was about to be broken up."

It sounds like a gruesome piece of advice—but, as far as finding personal significance goes—learn how to float!

LEARN NOT ONLY JUST TO FLOAT—but to FLOAT for <u>extended periods of time.</u>

What we are never told—or are told but don't key in on is: No matter who you are—you are going to have to float from time to time. Most of the time, you will be floating a lot longer than you want to!

> # Not just FLOATING—but floating for extended periods!

It is often assumed that God doesn't want people to float. Then "cosmic" logic commences—either God doesn't want me to float and there is some kind of sin in my life, or God can't do anything to help me.

The logic is wrong because the assumption is wrong. The truth is—GOD LIKES TO SEE US FLOATING!

When things are going great we assume we are doing everything right—which is often incorrect. Even when things are going great we could be doing some things that we shouldn't be doing, but because of the outcome we don't think anything more about it. It isn't until we are floating around—and holding on for dear life—are we interested in listening for improvement and development. HENCE: GOD LIKES IT WHEN WE ARE FLOATING!

God likes us to float because He knows we are listening better to Him.

Floating brings out the best (and worst) in all of us. We learn where both our strengths and weaknesses are. Most importantly, floating gives us time and opportunity to learn how to locate that place on the inside where we can find personal significance.

The only hope we can have about floating is—we float long enough out there to learn everything we can about ourselves.

The wind is always a problem wherever you go.

Get used to it.

"But the Lord sent out a great wind on the sea."

The only predictable aspect about wind is it is unpredictable.

Sailors love the wind—but only if it is going in the direction they are.

A cool breeze on a warm day is refreshing—but truthfully—how often does that happen? Answer: NOT VERY!

Wind is fun when you fly a kite—but only at a certain point—getting the kite up...and down...and free from tangling is the work behind flying the perfect kite on the perfect day.

The winds are always a threat—expect it to be so!

Bottom line: The wind is always a potential threat. Get used to it—live with it—EXPECT IT TO BE SO. The sooner you learn to expect the wind to be a threat to any situation, the sooner you will learn that you never will be able to control the conditions around you.

The wind teaches us tremendous lessons about life. Just like the wind has the potential to always be a problem—similarly there will always be situations that will be a problem for certain people.

The wind teaches us tremendous lessons about our lives.

There are some people that handle certain problems in certain ways and everything ends up being okay. But—when other people try the same thing the same way—it doesn't work out the same way.

Situations that bring problems are as unpredictable as the wind. GET USED TO IT. Don't over-analyze it. Don't over-think it. Don't spend too much time on it.

All you have to do is do your best. Your best is good enough.

> # We have to believe our best is good enough—especially for right now—until we learn more from the situation.

The point is—if you spend your time trying to solve the unsolvable—if you did make things better you would think you could handle every situation (which is still a lie).

When you think you can control things you will never find personal significance because your significance will be based upon a lie. It will seem like significance, feel like significance, but will destroy your psyche the second reality sets in.

Our personal significance needs to be based upon something greater than our own skill, our own gifts, and our own abilities to solve problems or control situations. PERSONAL SIGNIFICANCE NEEDS TO BE BASED UPON <u>BEING</u> RATHER THAN <u>DOING</u>!

This same concept is the template to other potential problems—like people. People can be as unpredictable as the wind. There may be some people who will always be a problem for you. Get used to it. Live with it. Don't try to always be getting people to like you—or believe it is always possible. The minute you believe it for a second is the minute you won't be able to find personal significance—because—you will believe your significance is based upon how people like you.

PERSONAL SIGNIFICANCE IS NOT BASED UPON WHO LIKES YOU OR NOT—BECAUSE PEOPLE ARE AS FICKLE AS THE WIND!

Finding significance is a basic need we all have. If you allow yourself the belief that if I try hard enough I can actually please others, you will be filling your life up with emptiness. People are insecure which makes them fickle (at best). If you base your significance in life on pleasing people or keeping certain people happy—your personal significance will be as fickle as the people you are trying to please.

People are as unpredictable as the wind. Get used to it. Learn to expect it. Train yourself never to allow yourself to find significance in what others think of you—or you are in for a huge disappointment. (In emotional terms you would be setting yourself up for a train wreck)!

Scan your surroundings to see what will hold your body weight.

"And there was a mighty tempest on the sea."

Now is the time for some good, honest personal analysis.

These are two important questions that will help you float better. They are also ones (as long as you are brutally honest with yourself) that will help you in the endeavor to find personal significance.

- **WHAT CAN I GRAB HOLD OF IN MY LIFE THAT WILL HELP ME FLOAT?**

The things that will help you float are also those things which will help you find personal significance in your life.

> # The things that don't help me float could pull me down!

The things that don't help you float may not cause you to drown, but may wear you out and zap your energy to float.

38

Any thing in your life that doesn't contribute to helping you float will never help you find personal significance.

If you ask yourself the question sincerely you will come up with the type of truth that creates the question—"NOW WHAT DO I DO?" (Maybe even with a little panic).

Don't over-react to what you find when you think about what may pull you down—just remember to let go of it when you are forced to float for long periods of time. If you don't let go—you deserve what you get!

The thing to do is NOT TO PANIC. If you realize there are things in my life that are pulling me down or could pull me down—the answer is not to be impetuous—but realize where the threat is.

The whole purpose of this exercise is if the time comes that you have to hold on to something to help you float you will know what to let go of.

- **WHO CAN I HOLD ON TO WHO WILL HELP ME FLOAT?**

This may be even harder to analyze—ask yourself who in your life will/would help you float—not pull you down?

This question should be simple to answer, but hard to face.

The reason the answer is simple is because the people who will help you float are those in your life who help you succeed right now.

The people who will pull you down are those who are pulling you down right now.

What should you do with this information? You don't have to throw people out of your life—but you should at least know where you should turn in the case of an emergency.

Further, the people who help you to float are also those people who will help you find personal significance. Those who are pulling you down—will never contribute to helping you find personal significance. They may even work against it!

Always be prepared to float—without being paranoid.

"So that the ship was about to be broken up."

You can always find a ship going in the direction you want to go—but—winds can tear your ship apart. So—always be prepared to float!

In the realm of finding personal significance, we should always be of the attitude that I will do whatever is necessary to find significance whether that means riding on a real nice ship or floating (holding on for my dear life).

Further, we shouldn't be paranoid about anything we face. Enjoying the ship, the ride, or the moment means we aren't being pessimistic or negative about when the next wind might whip up or calamity happen.

> We can enjoy something more fully if we can identify what will help us to float.

41

There is always a mentality we can apply to our lives which says—I really enjoy this thing or that thing, but if my ship goes down I'm not foolish enough to think this or that will help me float.

I enjoy the things around me—but these things that don't float (and there are plenty of them) DON'T GIVE ME PERSONAL SIGNIFICANCE.

We can apply the same thing to the people around us as well. Without being paranoid or insincere we can be honest with ourselves and know who around us can help us to float or pull us down with them. The honesty we put into our analysis will be the thing that helps us the most. As long as we can tell who will help us float we can tell who will help us find personal significance.

> It isn't hard to tell who will help you float or pull you down because they are doing it right now.

Those who pull you down should not be allowed to determine your significance in the world. The people who don't help you float, will generally do just the opposite. They will be the people who cause you to question whether or not you have any significance at all.

Knowing who—is the key to knowing "what"—which in this case is in helping you find your personal significance.

Thoughts to Ponder

- Floating for extended periods of time helps us find personal significance.

- The only thing predictable about the wind is that it is unpredictable.

- Get used to the wind—it will always be present in your life.

- Personal significance is based upon being rather than doing.

- What can I grab hold of in my life that will help me float?

- Who can I grab hold of in my life who will help me float?

- Expect the unexpected—always be prepared to float.

- The people or things that don't help me to float will never help me find personal significance any way.

- People or things that would pull me down when trying to float are pulling me down RIGHT NOW!

Chapter 4: "What You Do in a Crisis Defines You" 1:5

[5]"Then the mariners were afraid; and every man cried out to his god, and threw the cargo that *was* in the ship into the sea, to lighten the load. But Jonah had gone down into the lowest parts of the ship, had lain down, and was fast asleep."

Who you really are is never revealed until you face a crisis—then the real you appears.

What often happens is—we can give people advice and counsel all day long until something happens in our personal lives and it is a different story.

Do you really practice what you preach? More than a pithy question--this should give us some personal analysis that often slips past.

When we give advice, ask yourself: "Do I practice my own advice? Could I do what I just told this person to do?"

A crisis can help you find personal significance if you are ready to let it help you with your life. By this we allow the crisis to bring out who we really are and then take the time and energy to interpret our reaction to a crisis.

We face different levels of fear every day.

"Then the mariners were afraid"

We face various levels of fear every single day. Some of the fear is healthy, some of it is unhealthy.

Healthy fear is the kind that inspires you not to walk across the street without watching out for vehicles—you are "afraid" of hurting yourself.

At the same time, it is unhealthy fear that keeps us paralyzed from moving forward and stymied from advancement. This kind of fear keeps us fearful of just about everything—we fear failure; we fear what people are thinking about us; we fear what people are saying (or might say) about us.

There are also fears we bring with us from childhood. There are events that might have randomly occurred, but create fear in us to this day.

Fear is simply something we will face every day of our lives. The key is to face our fears—analyzing the power it has or the way it is controlling us—and then managing it by talking ourselves through it. In this way, personal significance can become a large part of our lives!

Monitor your own reactions—it reflects who you really are.

"And every man cried out to his god"

If we could only video tape ourselves—we would be quite surprised at our reaction to fear. (We would be quite surprised at our reactions in general).

We don't conduct ourselves the way we think we do—most of the time. Making a conscious effort to monitor our own selves is the only way to realize how we do react. Seeing yourself for who you are in a crisis is the most important way to seeing yourself for who you are. Additionally—you can see how you are defined—because you can now honestly take a look at yourself.

Looking at yourself in this way is a huge step toward finding personal significance because all of the façade and veneer used to cover up who you are is stripped away. Moreover, monitoring your reactions to things is just a good way to conduct your life. It keeps you accountable for your behavior and purposeful in your direction.

> **What you say and do during a crisis is what you would (actually) say and do.**

A crisis will bring out the truth about the object of your *worship*, what you really *value*, and how you really *feel*.

"And threw the cargo that was in the ship into the sea, to lighten the load."

What you really believe is brought out during a crisis. What you cling to during a crisis is really the object of your worship (or your center).

A crisis brings out what you worship/believe in. It defines who you are—and helps in finding personal significance.

When a crisis comes the typical response is to lighten the load. What you throw overboard at the time of a crisis is part of what defines you.

The thing(s) you throw overboard has much to say as to what is disposable to you. In a crisis, your mind will go right to it.

What you throw over to lighten the load reveals how you really feel about things in your life. Knowing this and gaining awareness of it will help you find personal significance.

A crisis will bring out your true mental condition—and if you need to attend to it or seek some help.

"But Jonah had gone down into the lowest parts of the ship, had lain down, and was fast asleep."

Sleeping is one of the best remedies for every kind of health need. Physically and mentally we need rest.

Excessive sleeping is a sign of a deeper problem. More than just exhaustion—sleeping to Jonah's level is a symptom of mental illness. Hindsight being 20/20, we see this is a problem with Jonah a couple of times in his story.

A crisis has a way of bringing out exactly what a person's mental condition is. From that point, we can do something about the illness.

The mind is not unlike the body when it comes to getting it into shape. Never should we think there is nothing that can be done. There is plenty to watch for when it comes to proper mental and emotional balance. Proper mental/emotional condition is essential in finding personal significance—so it is important to be aware of those such things that will threaten (and even destroy personal significance).

Hence, denial leads to depression.

Depression as a mental illness is no laughing matter. We shouldn't be making a diagnosis of someone's behavior (and especially from a four chapter story of about a month in a life) but Jonah seems like a person battling depression, manic/depressive disease, or other forms of illness.

Illness is an obstacle to finding personal significance—but—if a person can find significance in the face of illness, the result becomes a powerful force in one's life.

The world doesn't stop for anyone's illness. We need an awareness of this so we won't let our world stop for our illness!

> **The world doesn't stop for anyone's illness. We should be so aware of this that we won't let our world stop for our own illness!**

What we do in a crisis is what defines us as a person. Even in the face of a crisis a person can still find personal significance.

Thoughts to Ponder

- **Do you practice your own advice?**

- **There are events that may have randomly occurred, but creates fear in us to this day.**

- **The key is to face our fears by analyzing the power it has or the way it is controlling us—and then managing it by talking ourselves through it. In this way, personal significance can become part of our lives!**

- **What you cling to during a crisis is really the object of your worship (or your center).**

- **What you throw over to lighten the load reveals how you really feel about things in your life.**

- **Proper mental/emotional condition is essential in finding personal significance—so it is important to be aware of those such things that will threaten (and even destroy personal significance).**

Chapter 5: "All Hands Should Always Be On Deck" 1:6

[6]"So the captain came to him, and said to him, "What do you mean, sleeper? Arise, call on your God; perhaps your God will consider us, so that we may not perish."

Personal significance can never be found through laziness.

Sleeping through something important neutralizes one's personal significance and seriously jeopardizes future potential.

"All hands on deck" is not just about NOT sleeping through something either—it means to be <u>focused</u> and <u>attentive</u> while doing whatever it is you do. Finding personal significance requires a person to have enough desire for significance, that it becomes a "drive" for personal significance. This drive specifically squashes out any form of laziness.

> **Finding personal significance requires a person to have enough desire for significance that it becomes a "drive" for finding personal significance!**

All hands should always be on deck. It is the leader's responsibility to insure it—"So the captain came to him and said to him..."

There is no shirking of duty when it comes to participation. It is always the leader's responsibility to make sure everyone is on deck and accounted for—whether a teacher, an employer, a partner, a spouse, or a parent—everyone needs to be present.

If you let people sleep in, drift off, space out, or not pay attention—it is on the leader.

If the child is lazy—it is on the parent for letting it happen.

If the employee isn't productive—it is on the employer for letting it happen.

If the speed limits and traffic signs are disregarded—it is on the police for letting it happen.

People need their leaders to keep them on task and accountable. This is just how it works. Finding personal significance is only possible for people if they learn to be a good follower before becoming a leader.

A great follower makes a great leader—and a terrible follower makes a terrible leader. Leading and following both come into play with significance.

All hands should always be on deck. People who hide need help (not babied). The healing comes from being on deck—"What do you mean, sleeper?"

People who are hiding don't need to be babied—they need to be challenged.

It is often thought that people who are hurting should retreat and lick their wounds—but as long as they do that they will always be hurting.

It is uncomfortable to confront a hurting person—yet—it is their only hope of healing. They need to have someone help them see that as long as they remain in the "phase of hurting" the healing will never begin. Also, as long as you remain "hurt" you will never find personal significance in your life.

Healing can never begin until you quit allowing yourself to be babied—or expect to be babied by others.

All hands should always be on deck—it keeps you alert—"Arise."

The old adage goes—"if you don't use it you will lose it." The same is true of sleeping when everyone else is on deck—if you aren't on deck with the rest, you will become sluggish and unfocussed.

Staying on deck keeps you alert. When you are alert you learn more and increase your potential.

When you are alert, you increase your capacity to find personal significance in your life. If you stay below deck sleeping or feeling sorry for yourself, you cut off this capacity completely.

Most people who have been below deck sleeping and then "arise" to where everyone else is, regret the time they spent being tentative about surfacing.

True—there is plenty of time spent on deck where nothing happens. It can be boring and demanding—but you have a larger capacity for finding personal significance on the deck than below it.

> **The deck of a ship can be a boring and demanding place to be—but you have a much better chance of finding personal significance on the deck than below it.**

All hands should always be on deck—it keeps you aware of what is going on so that you will be closer to God—"call on your God."

God always wants to be closer to you—so why don't you want to be closer to God?

Is He too demanding? Is it too hard? Does He expect too much? The reasons vary—rarely do we own up to what we really think about God's requirements. Usually we blame what we hear about God's demand for obedience on man's personal interpretation and make God out to be whatever we decide He should be.

A person could go through life making God out to be whatever he/she wanted God to be—but without ever finding personal significance. *Just like Jonah—no one ever finds personal significance apart from God.*

The concept every person has to come to terms with is: I EXIST TO SERVE GOD HE DOESN'T EXIST TO SERVE ME!

> **No one can ever find personal significance apart from God in their life!**

All hands should always be on deck. No matter who you are, there are people depending on you to be on deck with them—"perhaps your God will consider us, so that we may not perish."

The ultimate truth about significance is—YOU ARE SIGNIFICANT IF PEOPLE ARE DEPENDING UPON YOU—and—the people on deck (while you are sleeping down below) ARE DEPENDING ON YOU!

You don't like the people on deck depending on you? It doesn't really matter as far as personal significance goes—YOU ARE SIGNIFICANT.

Further—if you are significant—what does it matter whether they like you or you like them? They are depending on you—you are significant to them—so wake up, get up, and head to the deck for further orders!

People on the deck are depending on you—and if someone is depending on you it makes you significant. (Whether you like the people who are depending on you or not).

Thoughts to Ponder

- Finding personal significance is never possible when there is laziness.

- Desire for personal significance must become a drive for personal significance.

- If a person is allowed to sleep during an important moment—it is the leader's responsibility.

- People don't need to be babied—they need to be challenged.

- The deck can be a boring place—but you have a better chance at finding personal significance there than down below.

- I exist to serve God; He doesn't exist to serve me.

- People are depending on me on the deck—whenever someone is depending on me I am significant.

Chapter 6: "The 'Why' is Always More Important Than the 'What'" 1:7-8

[7]And they said to one another, "Come, let us cast lots, that we may know for whose cause this trouble *has come* upon us." So they cast lots, and the lot fell on Jonah. [8]Then they said to him, "Please tell us! For whose cause *is* this trouble upon us? What is your occupation? And where do you come from? What is your country? And of what people are you?"

The reason behind anything that happens is more important than the event that happens.

The motive behind the action is always more important than the action—the reason is: You can change behavior, but only after understanding the reason for the behavior.

If all we do is punish behavior, all we are doing is treating the "symptoms" of the problem—not the actual problem.

Finding personal significance is about the "why" not about the "what." No one will ever feel significant if they are doing things to please others—because they know within themselves they are doing something that is outward, not inward.

Significance is first an inward ideal—not an outward one!

FAULT FINDING

Fault finding is brutalizing—it is better to equip, develop and nurture people—not control them.

"And they said to one another, Come let us cast lots that we may know for whose trouble has come upon us."

More time is spent on finding out whose fault something is than ever trying to help the person who is at fault.

Most of the time we want to find whose fault something is so we can get the responsibility off our own backs. Then—we discard the person at fault. What we don't realize is—every time we do this we are feeling less significant ourselves!

Finding fault is brutalizing—and kills any possibility for finding personal significance.

IT IS SO MUCH BETTER TO DETERMINE TO BE AN EQUIPPER OF PEOPLE—NOT A FAULT FINDER OF THEM.

A person who is equipping doesn't take the time to determine or assess fault because they are too busy trying to equip people to be better people.

People who equip others don't even see the need to find fault in others—they are actively trying to help others become better in their lives—while fault finders seek to make people feel worse about their lives.

There is something an equipper does that is important—they find out what the source of the problem was. Rarely is the source of the problem ever a person—and when it is—an equipper deals with the problem as the problem, not a person as the problem.

It is important to find the source of a problem so it can be targeted for a change. In this way, change can be positive and powerful—helping people find their personal significance along the way!

IT IS SO MUCH BETTER TO DETERMINE TO BE A NURTURER OF PEOPLE—NOT A FAULT FINDER OF THEM.

Nurturing people requires us to give direction and provide for meeting needs. It doesn't mean to cuddle or baby them (which are the last thing people need).

The bottom line: Don't control or be controlled by anyone or anything but GOD. God is the ultimate source for finding personal significance and the ultimate discourager from people finding fault in one another or in situations they face in their lives.

CALM DOWN & HOLD STEADY

If you hold steady a little while the truth always comes to the surface as long as the pot doesn't keep getting stirred up.

"So they cast lots and the lot fell on Jonah."

It doesn't take much truth in any situation—even just a little—and it will rise up in any environment.

Truth always has a way to rise to the surface in any and every situation. For this to be so—EVERYONE HAS TO CALM DOWN AND HOLD STEADY.

The reason everyone needs to calm down is because if the "pot gets stirred up" the truth won't have a chance to rise to the top.

The best illustration is of the rich part of cow's milk. Back before the day of huge dairy operations, dietary concerns, and pasteurization—farmers would get their cream through an over night process. Instead of stirring the milk they let it set over night. By morning there would be a heavy coating on top of their milk. This is the milk fat that we know of as the cream that usually gets mixed into whole milk for the richer taste (richer than skim milk).

The heavy coating would be skimmed off the top and used in coffee, on cereal, in making butter, ice cream and dozens of other things.

When it comes to finding the truth the same principle applies:

- Let the truth (even the smallest amount of truth) rise to the top.

- The only way for this to happen is for everything to calm down, settle down, and hold steady.

- Most importantly: Don't let anyone or anything stir the pot or the truth will get mixed up with everything else and not emerge.

This principle is universally applicable when trying to find out the "why" not the "what" of any situation.

Truth is the core of finding personal significance. You can't obtain personal significance without truth—but—it doesn't take much to find it.

PERSPECTIVE

Perspective gets skewed when God is left out of the picture—

"They said to him, please tell us"

If God is not at the center of something—then whatever else replaces God becomes the source for all perspective.

Personal perspective towards something gets skewed more than anything else in one's life.

If God is not at the center—then skewed perspective is the basis for whatever else life is built upon. People have vastly different perspectives at every turn—but if God is not the foundation for one's perspective then things could end up tragically for someone. (This is what would happen to Jonah because the men on the ship didn't have God as their center).

When God is the center of things then perspective is often the mutual point of communication and success. When perspectives differ (in this scenario) things don't have to end—but simply be worked out. People <u>without</u> God at their center are self-absorbed.

UNDERSTANDING

There is a deeper level of understanding that we don't access because we think too much and too highly of ourselves:

- "For whose cause is this trouble?"
- "What is your occupation?"
- "Where do you come from?"
- "What country?"
- "From what people?"

For whose cause is this trouble?

Does it really matter? For purposes of our lives and living we need to understand that it doesn't matter whose trouble it is—but that someone is having some trouble.

Who caused the trouble?—is a question we often ask when we are paying the price because of someone else. The truth is—it doesn't matter—because if I am keeping my nose clean and doing my best, I can out last, out think, and out work—the trouble.

A person desiring to find personal significance must accept things as they come. Trouble is part of life—it is something to grow from and find significance through.

What is your occupation?

What a person does is usually how he/she is identified.

A sense of destiny and identity are tied to what it is he/she does for a living.

The tragedy is a person whose identity is based upon what he/she does is a person who never truly finds personal significance.

It takes a lot of mental effort to keep oneself from allowing the sense of what you do to be your significance.

If you allow your identity to be your occupation, it may just work for you—but only for a little while—because when your occupation is taken away, your significance will be taken away as well.

Every person should find balance and moderation in life.

Be defined by your ethics, your honesty, your fairness, and your kindness as a person—not by your occupation.

The legacy a person leaves is something everyone considers—what will they say about me or think about me when I am gone? The idea of a legacy is what personal significance is all about.

Where do you come from—what country—what people?

The questions of identity are always important when it comes to personal significance because it brings issues to the surface.

Where you come from doesn't matter when it comes to personal significance—but often matters to you personally. Because it matters to you—it is important to come to terms with your background.

There are often negative associations made to where people come from. Yet—each person must realize where he/she comes from only defines him/her as a person as much (or as little) as he/she wants it to be.

Where you come from should only be considered a positive in your life. If there are negative connotations to your background realize that you have risen above it through finding personal significance. If there is a positive connotation from where you came from—it is all the better.

> **Where you come from should always be a positive thing—or turned into a positive thing!**

Thoughts to Ponder

- The motive behind the action is always more important than the action itself.

- It is much better to be an equipper of people—not a fault finder of them.

- People who equip others don't find the need to be a fault finder.

- When God is not at the center of your life—perspective always gets skewed.

- Who is causing the trouble shouldn't matter nearly as much as "I'm going to make it through this situation anyway."

- Who you are shouldn't have anything to do with your occupation.

- Where you come from shouldn't matter to your personal identity.

- If where you come from is not a positive thing—then turn it into a positive thing.

Chapter 7: "Confession is a Start but Only Comes When You Bottom Out" 1:9

[9]So he said to them, "I am a Hebrew; and I fear the LORD, the God of heaven, who made the sea and the dry *land*."

An Important Life Changing Confession Includes:

1. Confess who I am—"I am a Hebrew"

2. Confess who or what is the center of your life—"and I fear the Lord"

3. Confess the range of control your object of worship has over you—"the God of heaven"

4. Confess the power that object of worship has over you—"who made the sea and the dry land."

Confession (sincere and real confession) is the start to finding personal significance in your life.

Confession is the depth of the soul coming to terms with one's place and position in the world—it rarely comes unless something happens that causes a person to come to the end of self. It is at this point that a person is open to what is wrong—what went wrong—and how to fix it.

Confess who I am—"I am a Hebrew"

There are huge differences between a person who knows who they are and a person who doesn't.

The person who knows who he/she is—is secure in him/herself—confident in personal abilities—not intimidated by others—kind toward people—and doesn't take him/herself too seriously.

The person who doesn't know who they are is insecure—intimidated by people and situations—tentative about life—always worried about something/everything—and generally unhappy.

The purpose of this confession is to come to grips with who you are—I am who I am. I can't do anything about who I was born as—but I can do something about who I am turning out to be.

Yet—I have to confess who I am—so that I can hear myself say it.

I can't do anything about how I was born—but I can do something about who I am turning out to be!

Confess who or what is the center of your life—"and fear the Lord"

The first thing to do is to determine what your center is—then confess it. Coming to terms with what is at your center is the difficult part for most people.

The reason being: Coming to terms with what is at your center requires absolute honesty with yourself. The questions to ask yourself are soul-searching:

- What do I think about the most? That identifies what is at the center of your mind.

- What do I spend my time on/with the most? Whatever it is that consumes your time is at your center.

- What do I spend the most of my money on? The answer to this question identifies your most treasured possession and influences greatly what is at your center.

When looking over your answers, find the thing(s) that are the most repetitious—this will truly be the thing at the center of your life.

Now—confess what you have identified as your center. If it isn't God, it will reveal to you why you are having the difficulties you are having. If it is God—this will underscore your desire to find personal significance in your life.

Confess the range of control your object of worship has over you—"the God of heaven"

There are three dynamics that are important when dealing with the range of control of your object of worship.

Most people aren't able to define the range of control because they are often controlled by things that aren't beneficial to their lives. When this happens, the range of control becomes a blurred mess.

DEFINING THE RANGE OF CONTROL SOMETHING HAS OVER MY LIFE:

1. How much attention does it take? The object of one's worship is in need of more attention—how much does your object of worship consume?

2. How much attention do I give it? Come on now—let's be honest—or this exercise won't work!

3. What is the right range of attention and energy for me? How encompassing is the object of my worship? What are its demands of me—requirements of me—needs of me?

No matter what your object of worship is—it is important to come to grips with these ideas.

Confess the power the object of worship has over you—"who made the sea and the dry land"

Start off with observing how much power the object of worship has to begin with—then search yourself to see how much power it has over you.

The difference between the power something has in general and the power it has over you should be a revealing testament to whether you have a good thing or a bad thing as the object of your worship.

If something has ultimate power—then it should have ultimate power over me—because that is what was intended.

If something has limited power—but has a huge power over me—then something needs to be addressed in my personal life. I have let something get out of hand and out of balance.

The importance of confessing this is to get things going in the right direction. It helps you determine where you stand in regard to the object of your worship.

Either become more intense or change the object of your worship—the confession helps you find personal significance.

Thoughts to Ponder

- Confession (sincere and real confession) is the start to finding personal significance in your life.

- Confession is the depth of the soul coming to terms with one's place and position in the world.

- Coming to terms with what is at your center requires absolute honesty with yourself.

- I must be able to define the range of control something has in my life.

- Start off with observing how much power the object of worship has to begin with—then search yourself to see how much power it has over you.

- If something has ultimate power—then it should have ultimate power over me—because that is what was intended.

- If something has limited power—but has a huge power over me—then something needs to be addressed in my personal life. I have let something get out of hand and out of balance.

Chapter 8 "Everything Comes Down to 'What Do We Do Now'" 1:10-11

[10]Then the men were exceedingly afraid, and said to him, "Why have you done this?" For the men knew that he fled from the presence of the LORD, because he had told them. [11]Then they said to him, "What shall we do to you that the sea may be calm for us?"—for the sea was growing more tempestuous.

Everything in life has a starting point. It is that moment you can remember and come back to. If the starting point gets a little "fuzzy" in your mind—you need to revisit it once in a while.

In this way, everything needs a starting point. Make the starting point "the" point of anything you begin.

Finding personal significance is no exception to this principle of life. Everyone needs a starting point in finding personal significance—otherwise—you will spin your wheels and waste a bunch of your life in what will become an elusive endeavor.

How do we find a starting point? Everything in life comes down to it—WHAT DO WE DO NOW? The words that come after this question are the starting point of anything in your life!

The story of Jonah gives us the ideal model to developing a perfect starting point—that is—one you can come back to again and again.

The story of Jonah gives us the ideal model to developing a perfect starting point—that is—one you can come back to again and again.

What do we do now?

First: GET CONTROL OF YOURSELF!

"Then the men were exceedingly afraid"

If you don't manage your own emotions—you can be sure: Your emotions will manage you!

Emotions might even do more than just "manage you" they might even control your life.

Each person needs to find the way that works best in managing emotions. Whether the managing is to give yourself a pep talk, put a rubber band around your wrist and snap it, or deprive yourself of something—controlling yourself is the "starting point" of the starting point.

For many of us, seeing the danger of uncontrolled emotion is enough to get started with learning to control them.

Observe others and you will see some people who do well with managing their emotions—and others who don't. People who haven't learned to manage their emotions are people who haven't seen the damage uncontrolled reactions, outbursts, and behaviors can cause.

Emotions are not a bad thing. Everyone has emotions—it is part of being a human being. Just like nerve endings are important to the body—emotions are important to the mind.

The truth is: No emotional response can be just as bad as an uncontrolled emotional response. That is why it is called "managing" your emotions—not—no emotions at all.

Uncontrolled emotions skew the real picture of situations. It is hard to determine anything if the emotional level is heightened; even if one person isn't managing the emotional response in the circumstance.

Unmanaged emotions can drastically complicate situations. A starting point requires emotions to be managed. Personal significance requires emotional control—or personal significance is not possible. A person with uncontrolled emotions is too "needy" to find personal significance in life.

What do we do now?

Second: GET DOWN TO BUSINESS!

"And said to him"

There comes a time when you have to get down to business. People put this off for all kinds of reasons. Generally speaking, procrastination comes down to fear of the unknown. We become so accustomed to the inactivity that it becomes comfortable to us. Even the promise of a better life isn't motivation enough to get down to business.

Pain works the same way. We become accustomed to it—and living with pain becomes a way of life. Pain and hurt are what we know and we have embraced it for so long we don't know any better. The "starting point" is when we realize we don't have to live this way any longer.

Getting down to business is a decision—a personal decision.

Making the decision to get down to business is actually a great model in making the decision to get back to a starting point.

Getting down to business means several positive things to a person who needs a starting point in his/her life (in finding personal significance):

- Getting down to business means I'm going to cut through all the (crap) and start being <u>more direct</u> with myself and others. Many people waste their time going through other people's hoops, requirements, and "red tape" instead of getting down to business.

- Getting down to business means I am going to <u>move forward</u> in all areas of my life. The ability to move forward first requires a starting point to move forward from—get down to business and it will all come together for you.

- Getting down to business means honesty in every respect. Cutting through the "red tape" of living requires honesty. <u>Personal honesty</u> is the most disarming and beneficial attribute on the planet!

A positive life begins by always being able to relate to a starting point. The decision to "get down to business" is the moment anyone (everyone) can come to. All it requires is a decision!

What do we do now?

Third: STOP THE BLAME GAME—ALL IT DOES IS WASTE TIME!

"Why have you done this?"

The best thing we can do with blame in every context of our lives is to move through it quickly.

Finding the weak link in any endeavor is important but only to see where you need to be fortified—not to lay the blame on someone or some thing.

Blaming something is a "cop-out" in most contexts. It creates an environment that is inaccurate. Decisions are made and thoughts developed in this inaccurate atmosphere.

Because people fear rejection most of all—they would rather blame something than ever be open to sharing the blame. Finding something to blame gives us something to hide behind—hiding behind something—and hence, blaming something—hinders a person from finding personal significance in life.

79

Blame completely contradicts finding personal significance because you can't feel significant—you can't be significant if you made someone else insignificant—WHICH IS WHAT YOU DO WHEN YOU BLAME SOMEONE FOR SOMETHING!

Further, blame does more things that can cause great damage to the lives of people:

- Blame <u>creates an imbalance</u>. Everything in life has a balance except blame. There are many different names for the idea of balance—cause and effect; the ying and the yang; and so forth. There are many different (and shared) reasons for everything. No one is entirely to blame. Yet, blaming doesn't have a natural ability to share—but to access. This natural course gives blaming an imbalance in life.

- Blame <u>cops an attitude</u>. Whether you are the person doing the blaming or the one blamed, there is always attitude that goes before it, during it, and long, long after it. Attitude is important when it comes to logic because you can be absolutely right about something but if your attitude is wrong, you are wrong.

- Blame <u>always distracts</u> from the real issues. During blame, attitudes and counter attitudes are created. Soon, any semblance of the real issue is skewed and forgotten.

Fourth: ULTIMATELY, WE ALREADY KNOW WHAT TO DO—WE JUST HAVE TO DO IT!

"What shall we do to you that the sea may be calm for us?"

Many people are afraid of getting started with something because of the fear of failure. They would rather do nothing and maintain than to try something (even if it is the remotest possibility of failure).

Mistakes are part of life. Making a mistake does not mean you have failed.

The key is not in NOT MAKING a mistake—the key to life is in LEARNING something from the mistakes you make. As far as mistakes are concerned—how about adopting two goals:

- Learn from every mistake by not making the same mistake twice.

- Learn from every mistake by not making the mistakes I have seen other people make.

Every situation comes with a basic knowledge of knowing what you are supposed to do, (although you may have to get your emotions under control to realize it).

If you ever come to a point where you don't know what to do—it is because of one thing—you can't see the situation clearly through the intensity of your own uncontrolled emotional level.

The determination to help overcome the urging within to take it easy is to adopt this philosophy: I will be teachable in every circumstance I face:

- There is always something to learn—and I am going to learn it.

- I won't be scared off by the "what-ifs"—I am determined to learn from every "what if" I face in my life.

- I don't have to do it all perfectly. If I try I am sure it won't be close to perfect—BUT—it doesn't have to be!

When you blame, you are wasting your energy. When you know what you are supposed to do but don't "just do it" you are wasting your time.

Time is the most valuable commodity known to humankind. Why waste it if you don't have to?

What do we do now? One thing you <u>don't</u> want to do is burn bridges behind you as you go. We need to do the best we can at each of these levels to bring people along.

People move from what they know to what they don't know (known to the unknown). When people are hurt—they will get in your way because they are wounded. Try not to hurt them.

Be conscious of how you are coming across to people—it will go a long way on what their trust level is with you. This is important because those bridges we are tempted to burn are the same ones that will eventually be needed to get us back home!

What do we do now? It all comes down to that question. The answer: I'm going to start finding personal significance right now.

I'm going to start finding personal significance—right now!

Thoughts to Ponder

- Everything in life has a starting point. Everything in life needs a starting point.

- If you don't manage your emotions they will end up managing you.

- Every person needs to figure out how to manage his/her emotions.

- I need to simply "get down to business."

- Blaming is a waste of energy. It is a distraction from the real issues.

- Don't ever be scared off by the "what-ifs."

- Learn from every mistake. Make learning part of your life.

- Don't burn your bridges—you may need them to get back home.

Chapter 9:   "You Can't Get Anything Settled Until Someone Owns It" 1:12

¹²And he said to them, "Pick me up and throw me into the sea; then the sea will become calm for you. For I know that this great tempest *is* because of me."

Nothing gets settled until someone "owns it."

Owning it means someone accepts responsibility for whatever has happened.

Parents run into this when someone is naughty and they are trying to figure out how the naughtiness went down. Someone has to own up to the responsibility so the blame (and subsequent punish) is doled out properly.

Finding personal significance requires someone to own up to the responsibility as well. A person never experiences significance until they have first experienced what it means to "own it." If they don't own it, they will always feel guilty, never experience closure in any situation, or resolve differences.

Jonah's experience helps us to develop a model for "owning it." Through his situation we can see the importance that someone owning something has on the progress of situations we face in our personal lives—and further, in finding personal significance.

Owning something requires a person to step up—

"And he said to them"

Basically, a person who never steps up is likely never to find personal significance in his/her life—because he/she will always be too laid back and non-committal to discover what it means to be significant, do things that are significant, observe people of significance, or even participate in circumstances of significance.

Regardless of the circumstances you face—someone has to step up—otherwise all you have is a series of insignificant exercises. Significant progress will never be made.

How do I step up? It generally will depend upon the context that you are in at the time.

- I step up by admitting when I am wrong.

- I step up by asking for forgiveness or apologizing.

- I step up by granting forgiveness.

- I step up by letting something I am holding on to go.

- I step up by being the person to begin a conversation.

- I step up by being the first one to open up the dialogue concerning something.

- I step up by offering an apology even when I feel like I should be apologized to.

- I step up by being the person who tries to clear the air.

- I step up by confronting something directly, face to face—not behind people's backs.

- I step up by realizing I can be right about something, but if my attitude is wrong, I am wrong.

- I step up by analyzing how I am coming across to others—then taking the steps to better hone my communication skills.

- I step up by cutting other people slack and not being too critical of them or how they come across to others.

- I step up by giving people space and time to react and understand what is happening around them.

Owning something requires everyone around to accept what is happening—

"Pick me up"

There comes a point in the process of owning something that others have to come along to complete the process.

The person who "steps up" isn't the only one involving owning up. Stepping up is the start—the rest of it requires those involved to accept what is happening around them.

This is not something that can necessarily be rushed—but is always essential in resolution.

It is important to realize this because if the person who steps up begins to believe that just by stepping up the problem can be solved—then the "fix it" mentality can result. This is that belief that a person can go to work and fix any situation that arises.

The major problem with the "fix it" mentality is that manipulation can result because of the drive to fix whatever the problem is. Manipulation is never a problem solver.

Instead of trying to "fix it" by yourself—work together! Everyone involved should work in helping one another accept the circumstances.

Owning something requires group effort—

"And throw me into the sea"

People who find themselves in an associated relationship with one another have to find a way to work together.

Often we don't have a choice as to whom we are going to have to associate with, but we do have the choice to make it work or not once we are there.

Owning it requires group effort. Group effort happens by deciding we are going to make it work—one way or another.

It may be that people won't meet together half way—so part of the determination has to be that group effort. Group effort is so important that it may require going further than half way, if that is what is necessary to make it work.

No one can be left behind in this group effort. When people are left in the dust, someone does not own it—because "owning it" doesn't allow for individual effort only.

Actually, personal significance can be found through making the decision that no one is left behind and all matters will be resolved. The attitude is significant, the action is significant, and the result is significant!

Owning something is the best way for things to calm down—

"Then the sea will become calm for you"

Things will never calm down in any situation until people decide they are going to own it.

The process has to start with at least one person—but things won't progress unless others step up and join together to own a situation.

If things aren't calm in your life, you might consider that the problem is there because no one "owns" the situation. It has to start with someone—why not you?

You will never be able to find personal significance in your life unless things calm down. Chaos and confusion do nothing but prevent a feeling of significance.

> **You will never find personal significance in your life unless things calm down. There is never any significance during chaos or confusion.**

90

Owning something requires a person to just OWN UP—

"For I know that his great tempest is because of me"

Finding personal significance is like a doorway you have to walk through. It doesn't come after you—you have to walk through it to get to it.

The doorway for personal significance is when a person wanting to find it decides: I AM GOING TO OWN UP.

When a person decides to take responsibility, he/she walks through a doorway into a life of true significance. Until a person does this—there will always be a lack of personal significance in his/her life.

Owning up isn't without some pain. Taking responsibility can sometimes involve embarrassment, hurt feelings, or rejection. No matter what the price—finding personal significance (on the other side of the doorway) is always worth it!

No matter what the price, finding personal significance is always worth it!

Thoughts to Ponder

- Nothing gets settled until someone "owns it."

- Owning something means to accept responsibility for what has happened.

- Regardless of what is going on—someone has to step up and own it.

- I need to always be quick to offer a sincere apology.

- I need to always be quick to forgive and to ask for forgiveness.

- Stepping up can't be rushed—it is a process that takes time.

- Owning it is the quickest way to calm things down—something will not calm down until someone owns it.

- Owning it is just a start—others have to join the process as it goes.

- Owning it is like a doorway for personal significance.

Chapter 10: "Let it Happen—Then Deal with the Result" 1:13-16

[13]"Nevertheless the men rowed hard to return to land, but they could not, for the sea continued to grow more tempestuous against them. [14]Therefore they cried out to the LORD and said, "We pray, O LORD, please do not let us perish for this man's life, and do not charge us with innocent blood; for You, O LORD, have done as it pleased You." [15]So they picked up Jonah and threw him into the sea, and the sea ceased from its raging. [16]Then the men feared the LORD exceedingly, and offered a sacrifice to the LORD and took vows."

"Okay, let's just get it over with"—is the idea (and attitude) in this chapter.

All of us would say we can deal with just about anything except the unknown. The more the unknown lingers, the more exhausted we get. Dealing with the problem is not nearly as draining as wondering what the problem really is.

Patience wears thin while people wait around for "the other shoe to drop." (This is the idea that there is something more to happen before we can move on from this point).

> Let things happen—it is easier to deal with the result than the waiting around for it!

Resisting what you know you ought to do zaps your energy and frustrates everybody.

"[13]Nevertheless the men rowed hard to return to land, but they could not, for the sea continued to grow more tempestuous against them."

Going against what you know to be true about something—regardless of what it is—will always wear you out and leave you no where.

Plus: You will be much further behind in regard to finding personal significance.

On top of this—you will frustrate yourself and those around you by doing something that you know doesn't (or won't) work. Your heart just wouldn't be into it—and those around you know it isn't a sincere effort. Everyone gets frustrated under these conditions.

When your heart isn't into what you are doing the people around you know it—continuing on will frustrate them and you!

Guilt is a waste of time.

[14]Therefore they cried out to the LORD and said, "We pray, O LORD, please do not let us perish for this man's life, and do not charge us with innocent blood; for You, O LORD, have done as it pleased You."

Feeling guilty is just a waste of time—because—it never solves a problem or helps a situation.

Guilt is one of the most manipulative forces of all time.

People are insecure. They are always searching for ways to find personal significance. As a result, people are constantly prone to guilt.

Guilt is resolved when an individual decides he/she is going to act upon what they know, do their best, and let it go.

"POOF" GUILT IS GONE!

There are complications when people blame someone else for their situations; slack off and become lazy; or lack courage on acting on the knowledge they hold.

THE SOLUTION:

- Accept responsibility
- Work hard
- Be courageous

Just do it and deal with it.

"[5]So they picked up Jonah and threw him into the sea, and the sea ceased from its raging."

Do what you know you need to do. Don't second guess it, over-analyze it, or dawdle.

Once you have done what you need to do—then deal with the result.

It isn't just about wasted time. A lot of confusion can result when people spend time over thinking things rather than just getting it done.

Take away the scourge and distress you face by just tackling your issues head-on. It is the only way to go. Deal with it and then move on!

Don't second guess yourself, over-analyze, or dawdle!

Always cover your bases with God!

"The men feared the LORD exceedingly, and offered a sacrifice to the LORD and took vows."

Every person on the planet needs to figure out a way to be up to date in his/her relationship with God every second of his/her life.

There should never be a moment where a person feels completely alone. The truth is—as sad as it sounds—people often feel alone and isolated. A person who feels lonely, will never find personal significance because the loneliness is consuming.

It isn't until a person comes to terms with his/her relationship with God that he/she is ever able to deal with life—let alone the problems that emerge in life.

"Relationship" is more than a culturally popular term—it is the best way to describe God's desire for being with (and in) each of us.

God isn't watching us from a distance. He is in our lives—inside our minds—living in the center of who/what we are—and central in everything we will become. In this way, personal significance will never happen apart from God being in our lives at an intimate level.

Relax—quit worrying about stuff—if you open your life to God, He is in control of it all!

Thoughts to Ponder

- Let's get it over with!

- It is always easier to deal with the result than to wait around for it to happen.

- Going against what you know to do will always wear you out.

- When your heart isn't into something you will frustrate yourself—and those around you.

- People are insecure—they are always searching for ways to find personal significance—as a result—they are constantly prone to guilt.

- Do what you know you need to do. Don't second guess it, over-analyze it, or dawdle.

- Every person on the planet needs to figure out a way to be up to date in his/her relationship with God every second of their life.

- "Relationship" is more than a culturally popular term—it is the best way to describe God's desire for being with (and in) each of us.

Chapter 11: "God Protects, Preserves, and Provides—But Not the Way You Think" 1:17

[17]Now the LORD had prepared a great fish to swallow Jonah. And Jonah was in the belly of the fish three days and three nights.

The best way to view life is to expect the unexpected. In this way, you will never become too bored, or too scared about anything you face!

It is best to view the unexpected as a problem to be solved, not some insurmountable thing that can't be managed.

Finding personal significance requires us to believe that God preserves, protects and provides so that we can get our minds off our personal survival and on to our personal significance.

A great way you can find personal significance is to help others gain this same attitude over their personal survival.

Always expect the unexpected and you will never be bored or scared!

God Protects

¹⁷Now the LORD had prepared

God's protection is always a provision that is provided in plenty of time to keep us from harm. The only problem is—it doesn't seem like God's protection is there—because it comes in the very knick of time.

The whole point about God's protection is:

- It always comes in time.

- It always is just right for what the situation is.

- It always begins way before a problem began.

Because God doesn't live in just this present moment, but sees our lives like a train (from engine to caboose), He is able to make things come together for days, months, and years before it is necessary.

What we must get through to our thinking—(the thing we need to get our head around) is that God's protection is unconditional and automatic. I need not think about it. I don't need to go through some exercise or ceremony for His protection. I don't even need to believe in His protection (we can't be sure Jonah ever believed)—but it sure takes the edge off our concerns if we do.

When we can calm down and relax—we can get back to the real issue—finding personal significance in our lives.

God Preserves

"A great fish to swallow Jonah"

God preserves lives through preserving situations. We just couldn't guess that He would use a large fish to fulfill this purpose.

But then—we can never guess what God might be using to preserve our lives.

It was storming when Jonah was thrown over board. By the time he opened his eyes, he was surrounded by darkness. At first he wouldn't have known that this was the preservation of his life. He wouldn't have known where he was.

Our belief that God is preserving our lives should be so strong that when we end up like Jonah we assume that this is God's preservation.

Who would think there is a fish large enough to preserve someone's life? Who would think being swallowed by a fish is preserving someone's life? Who would believe anything so threatening would actually be the opposite?

If we can get our head around this we can be more relaxed and at ease to find personal significance:

God Provides

"And Jonah was in the belly of the fish three days and three nights"

Jonah stayed put until God had his full and undivided attention!

If situations resolve too quickly, we begin to think it was because of our own talent or skill. But when resolving them takes a little longer than we think—we get the idea that the power might have been greater than ourselves.

Our natural tendency is to get down to business, get things taken care of, and skip on to the next big thing. God wants something different—He wants us to learn as much as we can from every situation—that is why we are stuck there from time to time.

Jonah spent three days and three nights inside the big fish—he wasn't released from God's provision until all the lessons were learned.

God provides—every time. In return, He expects to have our undivided attention and energy to learn everything we can while He is making the provision for us.

Thoughts to Ponder

- The best way to view life is to expect the unexpected.

- The best way to view a problem is as something to be solved—not as an insurmountable situation.

- God's protection always comes just in time.

- It is important to believe in God's protection so that we can relax and focus our energy not on worry—but on finding personal significance.

- Our belief that God is preserving our lives should be so strong that when we end up like Jonah we assume that this is God's preservation.

- NO MATTER WHAT IT LOOKS LIKE, FEELS LIKE, OR SEEMS—THIS IS GOD'S PRESERVATION OF MY LIFE!

- The natural tendency is to get down to business, get things taken care of, and skip on to the next big thing. God wants something different—He wants us to learn as much as we can from every situation—that is why we are stuck in one place from time to time.

Chapter 12: "Anytime is a Good Time to Look to God" 2:1

[1]Then Jonah prayed to the LORD his God from the fish's belly

There is always "THE MOMENT" for everything (anything) that occurs in my life.

There are several ideas that come out of the idea of "the moment"—quite varied and coming at it at different levels of understanding.

- There is always a starting point to everything. We don't just "ooze" into something. There is always that one special moment.

- For circumstances to be resolved there is always "the moment" of crisis. The moment of crisis is very important in life. The crisis pertains to the realization that something new needs to happen. A crisis is important at every level of life: physical, emotional, and spiritual.

- We should always be tuned in so we don't miss that one special moment. That special moment isn't a secretive or sneaky thing, but it does require a person not to be so distracted by the situation that he/she misses the special moment. An example of this is the parent always videoing the family and missing that special moment of significance because they had one eye peering through a lens to record it.

There is that one moment—the moment that makes ALL THE DIFFERENCE. The moment occurs at the speed of thought—when I look to God—"Then Jonah"

Finding personal significance never happens apart from God. God's involvement starts at the very moment we look to Him for help.

Personal significance isn't the words we use, or the ritual we perform—it is about the heart. God is concerned with what is going on inside of us. It's not about what other people see—but how things really are on the inside.

Do drums roll or trumpets blast the moment I look to God? Not likely—but what will happen will be so profound human words cannot describe. I will experience peace that passes understanding—and personal significance that transcends comprehension.

All this because I looked to God for one simple moment!

The moment I look to God everything changes—and I begin to find personal significance.

There is that one moment—the moment when I realize I am over my head and have to reach out to God—"Prayed"

Is it alright to say that prayer is for people who are over their heads?

It may seem like prayer is for the weak—but the truth is: IF WE WERE TRULY HONEST ABOUT THIS—we all feel weak and over our heads on a pretty regular basis!

Some people have a struggle with coming to terms with being over their heads in a situation. People struggle because pride has guided them too long. People with a pride problem will sense the truest form of freedom when they realize they have to look to God—not themselves—for help and strength.

The moment I realize I am over my head and reach out to God is the most positive moment in my life.

Hopefully, the moment this happens the effect will be so powerful that finding personal significance will only feel like it is "one prayer away."

TRULY:
Personal significance is always just "one prayer away."

There is that one moment—that moment when I see that I need a higher power for my own good—"from"

And—my reaction to realizing my need for a higher power is—full and total surrender to God.

Further—the purpose for realizing my need of a higher power is full and total surrender to God.

But—the most important thing to remember is I am doing this for my own good!

The moment I see a need for a higher power for my own good is one that is remembered forever:

- Because it is my own special moment.

- It didn't happen because of pressure from others.

- It didn't happen because I was doing what someone else wants me to do.

- I was not mimicking someone else's life or life experiences.

Finding personal significance doesn't begin until one sees that they have a need for a higher power for their own good. Until that moment you are living someone else's life—not your own. Personal significance begins the moment your life starts to be your own!

There is that one moment—that moment where I realize my own thinking is all foolishness and because of it I end up in foolish places—"the fish's belly"

Here is a moment to remember forever—the moment I realize that I am not as smart as I thought I was!

When a person comes to terms with their own frailty, flaw, or failure—then begins the moment of growth. Until then, all we have is the capacity to blame others or deny our situation.

We don't ever have complete freedom until we realize:

- "I am flawed—sometimes it shows through"

- "I have failed—it isn't anyone else's fault"

- "I did my best—but even my best wasn't good enough"

- "I have been thinking/doing something foolishly—and now I must pay the price for it"

- "I have been denying the truth"

- "I have been blaming others"

- "I got what I deserved"

Maturity comes as we accept and grow from these kinds of situations. Plus—personal significance emerges out of the situations I face.

108

Thoughts to Ponder

- There is always "THE MOMENT" for everything (anything) that occurs in my life.

- We don't just "ooze" into something—because there is always that one special moment.

- We should always be tuned in so we don't miss that one special moment. The moment isn't a secretive or sneaky thing, but it does require a person to not be so distracted by the situation that they miss the special moment.

- Finding personal significance never happens apart from God—and God's involvement starts at the very moment we look to Him for help.

- Finding personal significance doesn't begin until one sees that they have a need for a higher power for their own good. Until that moment you are living someone else's life—not your own.

- When a person comes to terms with his/her own frailty, flaw, or failure—then begins the moment of growth. Until then, all we have is the capacity to blame others or deny our situation.

Chapter 13:   "The Prayer of Deliverance" 2:2-6

Is there such a thing as a prayer that brings me deliverance? Absolutely!

Anyone who gets swallowed by a large fish and is still alive to pray—must have something to teach us about how to be delivered through prayer.

The whole idea of a prayer of deliverance has as much to do about the situation to begin with as it does how to be delivered out of the situation.

There are no quick fixes or short cuts. We need to learn all we can about the situations in which we find ourselves.

When we do get out of a scrape without a scar—we shouldn't be happy—we should be concerned that we didn't absorb all we could. The easier it is to get out of a scrape, the more likely you are to fall back into it.

The prayer of deliverance serves as a powerful model for our lives. It is powerful because it is more than just some words or a chant—it is a testimonial of one's life—which is what prayer is supposed to be.

> ## The "Prayer of Deliverance" brings personal significance into my life!

#1—I'M IN TROUBLE

And he said:
"I cried out to the LORD because of my affliction,"

Only coming to God when you are in trouble is a problem—but the most important thing is to come to God!

The admission that "I'm in trouble" is the beginning point to finding a solution.

There is something that happens when a person admits he/she is in trouble that affects several levels of life:

- The harmful kind of pride has to be stripped away to admit you are in trouble.

- A vulnerability and transparency is developed that is necessary to be open for help.

- An approachableness surfaces that wasn't present before a person admitted he/she was in trouble.

- An over all openness to others is developed that provides an emotional ease and a disarming approach to life.

#2—BUT I KNOW GOD HEARS ME

"And He answered me."

God is listening—God is watching—God desires to be part of my life: These are all significant to the prayer of deliverance.

Unless a person believes God is present and cares—a prayer of deliverance has no more power than reading a poem to provide one a little comfort.

It is interesting: Most people forget about God, His care and deliverance, when things are going well for them. The moment something goes wrong they begin to pray and look to God.

The idea of the prayer of deliverance is to believe God is present all the time. I don't need to dial up some "special number." He is present and willing to help me all the time.

God doesn't have to do something to show me a "sign." God is not required to go through some special set of hoops to prove to me that He hears my prayer.

God is God—the creator of the universe. I EXIST TO SERVE HIM—HE DOESN'T EXIST TO SERVE ME.

#3—I'M AT MY END

"Out of the belly of Sheol I cried,"

The end is always the beginning! I'm in trouble, but I know God hears me—sounds like the end—but not until I confess: "I am completely at the end of my rope"—am I completely at the end of my rope.

The idea of "Sheol" that Jonah uses was his version of the land-fill (the place the garbage is taken). The community garbage has to go somewhere and the Hebrews set up a part of their community—outside the boundaries of their habitation to place and then burn their garbage and waste products. They called it Sheol. Jonah is saying that he is in the middle of a burning garbage dump.

He is at the end of himself. As impossible as it sounds—this is the best place to find yourself.

A person has more potential in his/her life when he/she is at the end—because anything out there is an improvement.

A person who is at the end of himself/herself is more open to help—and hence more open to rescue than any other time.

The end of self starts the beginning of something else. Don't hold back—when you are at the end—embrace it.

113

#4—YOU ARE THE ONLY ONE WHO CAN HELP ME

"And you heard my voice."

Anyone who is trying to find personal significance needs to have a singleness of mind when it comes to listening to the source and support of all things.

We are not just "covering our bases" when it comes to God. We believe He is the creator of the universe who desires to have a personal relationship with each individual.

The fruit of this personal relationship is my desire for God to be the only one who can help me. Any form of help I receive—I will acknowledge as coming from God—regardless of its source.

The resolve is—I don't regard any help as coming from anything but God and His providence.

As a person embraces this ideal—the result is a life of surrender and obedience to God—the fulfillment that comes from finding personal significance.

Believing, and then living, that God is the only one who can help me bring to life the true meaning of personal significance.

> **The belief that God is my help brings to life the true meaning to personal significance.**

#5—EVEN NOW I KNOW I AM RIGHT WHERE YOU WANT ME TO BE

[3] "For You cast me into the deep,
Into the heart of the seas,
And the floods surrounded me;
All Your billows and Your waves passed over me."

Coming to terms with where a person is at present is one of the most difficult parts of the prayer of deliverance.

Further—the key is to come to the same conclusion as Jonah which is: "I am right where I need to be."

"I am right where I need to be—I am right where God wants me to be right now." This is a powerful testimony to help relax and relieve the stress when one is need of deliverance.

The belief that—"I am right where God wants me to be"—gives each of us some remarkable opportunities:

- It gives me an emotional affirmation until something substantial does happen.

- It clears the way for my personal openness to what God wants to do with my life.

- It humbles me—taking away the destructive part of pride that comes from assumptions and presuppositions.

#6—THE HARDEST CONDITION IS TO BE OUT OF GOD'S PRESENCE

[4] "Then I said, 'I have been cast out of Your sight;
Yet I will look again toward Your holy temple.'
[5] The waters surrounded me, *even* to my soul;
The deep closed around me;"

The prayer of deliverance establishes something that is essential in deliverance—God's position in your life. It brings a person back to the basics.

The basic idea about the need for deliverance is to establish what the roughest condition really is—in life in general—and in a particular situation.

Boil the concept of deliverance down to the main thing. What is the most difficult situation in regard to deliverance?

Answer: The roughest thing is the feeling when I feel like God is not near.

Further—the only time I feel this way is when I am fully centered upon myself and no one or nothing else.

Then the conclusion hits me—keeping God at the center of my mind and my life and finding personal significance is <u>one and the same</u>!

#7—YOU HAVE MY ATTENTION AND I AM LISTENING

"Weeds were wrapped around my head.
⁶   I went down to the moorings of the mountains;
The earth with its bars *closed* behind me forever;"

This is the resolution part of being delivered:

- I am going to learn from my mistakes.

- I am going to go back over how I ended up here and resolve not to end up here again.

- I know I am supposed to be learning something—so instead of complaining I am going to embrace this experience and remember it.

- I resolve to listen better—to God, to others, to life and to myself.

- I am not going to totally disregard this experience and block it out. I am going to move forward.

The direction that comes when you need deliverance is usually clear because clarity comes as you are focused on something larger than yourself. There is an important truth to learn in this regard—you don't have to bottom out to remain focused through out your life.

#8—I WILL DO WHATEVER YOU WANT ME TO DO

"Yet You have brought up my life from the pit,
O LORD, my God."

- What is the ultimate goal in the prayer of deliverance?

- What is the ultimate place to start in finding personal significance?

These two questions are answered with one ultimate attitude:

"I will do whatever God wants me to do"—submission and surrender!

> The ultimate result comes down to the same thing—my personal resolution to be submitted to God. This is also the ultimate attitude to find personal significance!

Thoughts to Ponder

- The admission that "I'm in trouble" is the beginning point to finding a solution.

- The idea of the prayer of deliverance is to believe God is present all the time. I don't need to dial up some "special number." He is present and willing to help me all the time.

- A person has more potential in his/her life when he/she is at the end—because anything out there is an improvement.

- Anyone who is trying to find personal significance needs to have a singleness of mind when it comes to their source and support of all things.

- "I will do whatever God wants me to do"—submission and surrender!

- I am going to go back over how I ended up here and resolve not to end up here again.

Chapter 14: "Don't Forget to Remember" 2:7

⁷ "When my soul fainted within me,
I remembered the LORD;
And my prayer went *up* to You,
Into Your holy temple.

Remembering what you have been through in your life insures you don't have to keep repeating your mistakes.

Most cultures build huge monuments memorializing situations, circumstances, and events they have been through as a people.

It isn't necessary to go through the process of building some huge monument to remind us—but it is important to remember what we have been through in our lives.

> **It isn't necessary to build a huge monument to memorialize what you have learned as long as you just remember your mistakes!**

Don't forget to remember: The reason I am in trouble is because I became distracted.

But—

I have learned from it.

"When my soul fainted"

When you think of the times you were in trouble—always think in terms of the times you were distracted from what you were supposed to be doing.

Identifying the triggers to the trouble helps us to remember why we got ourselves into trouble.

If we can identify getting into trouble with becoming distracted—it should teach us that we should work to keep from getting distracted!

What are the things that distract you? Make yourself a list.

In what situations are you most vulnerable to distractions? If you can't avoid these situations completely, you should at least do them while you are freshest mentally. Otherwise you will be faced with that sluggish feeling that comes where you are the most vulnerable.

Everyone should be able to identify quickly what distracts them—and then avoid those situations and circumstances.

Don't forget to remember: The reason I am in trouble is because I made too much of it about me.

But—

I have learned from it

"Within me"

When a person begins to personalize things in the wrong way it becomes what is known as being "self absorbed." Everything ends up being "all about me."

When we make things about ourselves all kinds of negative attitudes and behaviors follow us: pride, defensiveness, sarcasm, scrutiny and others—there is no end to the negative life.

Self-absorbed living brings us trouble. It is not all about me.

Most things have nothing to do with me.

Whenever you find yourself feeling negative, on edge, or sensitive—think in terms of this challenge: QUIT MAKING IT ALL ABOUT ME!

> **Most things have nothing to do with me—so quit making it "all about me!"**

Don't forget to remember: The reason I am in trouble is because I forgot to always remind myself of God's track record.

But—

I have learned from it. "I remembered the Lord"

The point—God has a perfect track record. He hasn't ever messed up, made a mistake, or forgotten something.

By comparison—we are human beings and mess up all the time. We are flawed—God is not.

The reason we get ourselves in trouble is we get our own frailties and God's attributes confused.

There is nothing to worry about if you have turned something over to God—because He never messes things up.

There is nothing to worry about if you have turned something over to God—because now it is up to Him to deal with it.

There is nothing to worry about if you have turned something over to God—because He has a perfect track record in dealing with things.

Now I will let God worry about it!

Don't forget to remember: The reason I am in trouble is because I didn't pray, praise, worship, or equip myself better.

But—

I have learned from it. "And my prayer went up to You, Into Your holy temple"

When you are in trouble there is always plenty of time and opportunity to scold yourself about what you didn't do.

The real issue is one's personal resolve to do better—especially when talking about prayer, worship, and study.

Finding personal significance is all about prayer, worship, and equipping yourself in a deeply spiritual way. There are no short-cuts or quick fixes when it comes to developing in your spiritual life.

I will: Pray, worship, and equip myself better from this moment forward!

Thoughts to Ponder

- Remembering what you have been through in your life insures you don't have to keep repeating yourself when it comes to mistakes.

- Identifying the triggers to the trouble helps us to remember why we got ourselves into trouble.

- What are the things that distract me? Make yourself a list.

- When a person begins to personalize things in the wrong way it becomes what is known as being "self absorbed." Everything ends up being "all about me."

- The reason we get ourselves in trouble is we get our own frailties and God's attributes confused.

- There is nothing to worry about if I have turned something over to God—because He has a perfect track record in dealing with things.

- The real issue is your resolve to do better—especially when talking about prayer, worship, and study.

Chapter 15: "Making Worship—Worth It" 2:8-10

⁸ "Those who regard worthless idols
 Forsake their own Mercy.
 ⁹ But I will sacrifice to You
 With the voice of thanksgiving;
 I will pay what I have vowed.
 Salvation *is* of the LORD."

Finding personal significance is not all about me—even though the endeavor itself may seem to be!

The idea of worship is the establishment, in your very center, of a power greater than self. Finding true significance is not possible until this takes place. Also—unless this happens—any personal significance is not real significance, but only one's ego imitating the feeling of fulfillment enough it seems like significance.

Worship establishes a power greater than me at my center—thereby setting the stage for personal significance.

The thing I think about the most is the object of my worship!

"Those who regard worthless idols"

Every single person has something at his/her center—and it isn't hard to figure out what it is: It is the thing you think about the most.

The question you have to ask yourself is—"Does the thing at my center help me (or hurt) to find personal significance?" The answer to this question will guide you in this endeavor of finding personal significance.

Whatever is at your center will be the thing from which you will derive your personal significance. If you have a career at your center—your career will be where you will find your significance. Many people are happy this way—<u>but only for a short while</u>. Once the career is gone—so is your center—and so is your personal significance.

The same thing can be said about relationships. If you put a person at your center—you will derive your personal significance from him/her. If the relationship starts to weaken—or change—so will your personal significance.

You need to grow beyond the place where anything in the temporal world is your center because everything in this world changes. Finding true personal significance needs to be found in something more than a changing dynamic.

If you are really going to find personal significance—the real deal—it has to be built and based upon God.

The Hebrew people of the Old Testament provide an excellent source for study and analysis of this concept. Every time the object of their affection was on something other than Jehovah, everything fell apart. Whenever the people came back to God, things improved. God gave the Hebrews instructions to follow to help protect them and preserve their lives. When they followed God's instructions, they lived. When they didn't follow God's instructions, they died.

Finding personal significance has to be a life long endeavor. We grow and develop—stretch and succeed. This is only accomplished when we have God the center of our lives (our object of worship).

> **What you think about the most is your object of worship. What do you think about the most?**

I accept God's mercy upon me and will extend it to others as my worship!

"Forsake their own mercy"

Worship doesn't mean anything unless it makes a difference in my life—but—it doesn't stop there. Worship has to extend beyond my own life to have the impact it is intended to have.

God doesn't need more adulation or praise to make Him feel better about Himself. He needs it so we can feel better about ourselves (personal significance). How does this happen? It happens when we take the experience of putting God at the center of our lives—and finding personal significance and then extending myself to others.

Reaching out to others is actually part of the experience of worship. It is the completion of the cycle of worship. Further—true worship hasn't occurred until people reach out to help other people.

Extending mercy and compassion to others makes someone feel better about themselves—but unless God is at your center first it is only making you feel better about you—not about personal significance!

A thankful spirit keeps everything in check!

"But I will sacrifice to you with the voice of thanksgiving"

The spirit that matters most of all is to be thankful above all!

There is something that being thankful can do in your life that nothing else can. The impact a thankful spirit has is deep and instant.

Even when you are at the end of yourself, you can be thankful. Even when you are feeling sorry for yourself, you can be thankful. It is at these times it is called the "sacrifice of thanksgiving"—being thankful even when you don't feel like being thankful.

There is something life changing about sacrificing your spirit of thanksgiving even when you don't feel like it. It can turn any situation around RIGHT NOW—THIS VERY SECOND.

Most importantly—the spirit of thanksgiving is not derived from an emotion—but instead from a decision—the simple decision to be thankful.

Commitment is positive and life sustaining!

"I will pay what I have vowed. Salvation is of the Lord"

"Follow through" is the hardest process for most people. It also provides the richest opportunity for those wanting to find personal fulfillment.

"You get what you pay for" is one of the truest statements of all time. This same statement parallels what commitment means in sustaining a positive and growing life.

Growth is not possible without commitment. Making a commitment and sticking with it is what Jonah means when he says (while in the belly of the fish) "I will stick with my vow."

The moment of commitment is an important moment we should all capture for the future. The commitment is something we might have to go back to, just to remind ourselves, of what it is we said.

Sometimes reminding ourselves of our own commitment is all we have to help us stick with something to the end. Learning to stick with a commitment is essential in finding personal significance.

Thoughts to Ponder

- The idea of worship is the establishment of a power greater than self—and at your center.

- Every single person has something at their center—and it isn't hard to figure out what it is: It is the thing you think about the most.

- There is something that being thankful can do in your life that nothing else can. The impact a thankful spirit has is deep and instant.

- Reaching out to others is actually part of the experience of worship. It is the completion of the cycle of worship. Further—true worship hasn't occurred until people reach out to help other people.

- The moment of commitment is an important moment we should all capture for the future. It is something we might have to go back to (just to remind ourselves) of what it is we said.

Chapter 16: "Vomiting Something Clean" 2:10

^{10}So the LORD spoke to the fish and it vomited Jonah onto dry *land*.

If you haven't caught on to this yet—here it is: NEVER THE EASY WAY!

We shouldn't expect things to go smoothly and then we will never be disappointed. Most of the time—things won't (or don't) go smoothly. But then—finding personal significance is not about how smoothly things go.

Finding personal significance is, by its very nature, an endeavor pursued in the face of many conflicts. Conflicts are part of life—expect it and learn from it.

God caused the large fish to vomit Jonah out of its body and on to dry land. It sounds entertaining if it were a movie. For Jonah however, it was gruesome!

Just like the large fish was a place of protection for Jonah at a time when God was trying to speak to him—so vomiting him out was God's deliverance. Further, it was God's answer to Jonah's prayer. Hence, vomiting something clean can be God's answer!

Don't underestimate God's ability to use anyone or anything to accomplish His purpose for your life—"So the Lord spoke to the fish"

If God would speak to a fish—He will use anyone or anything to accomplish His purpose in your life.

There are so many times we get it into our heads where the answer is going to come—and thereby miss it when it really does come. It can be right before our eyes and never recognize it because we were not thinking of it.

There are also times when we miss the answer because we aren't expecting it. We get it into our thinking that our resource is in a paycheck, or person, or even winning the lottery that we forget God is our resource—not the money bags.

The problem is—if we are expecting the answer we often won't recognize it when it is right before our eyes.

Expect the Unexpected! How else would you know it is God?

Don't underestimate God's ability to make us uncomfortable—"and it vomited"

There is nothing comfortable about hearing what happened to Jonah at this point. Furthermore, thinking that this might be God's MO (Method of Operation) can make a person extremely uncomfortable.

Making us uncomfortable is God's specialty. It isn't until we are uncomfortable that we are paying attention to God in the first place.

When things are going well and we're feeling good, we think everything is fine. At the same time we think God is pleased with us. This attitude of being self-satisfied is harmful to us in that we feel that "comfortable" means God is pleased with us.

Uncomfortable is better by far. When we are uncomfortable we are listening better, thinking clearer, looking deeper, and hopefully surrendering ourselves to God.

Never underestimate God's desire to make us uncomfortable.

Don't underestimate God's desire for us to learn and grow from every situation—"Jonah"

There is always something to learn. God's desire—His expectation of us—is to learn everything we can every time we can.

<u>How</u> we learn something varies from person to person and from circumstance to circumstance. <u>What</u> we learn also varies from person to person.

The most important thing is not how or what—<u>the most important thing is that we learn.</u>

Jonah was learning as he went—so do we. Finding personal significance requires us to be students of life. Learn from every situation you face. Learn from every person you meet. (Even if you think you are smarter than the other person, there is always something they can teach you).

Personal significance is extremely important in your life if you learn from life—because it makes you more aware of the significance in everything that happens in life.

If you don't learn from people and situations you miss out on what life has to offer—and the thing you will never find is personal significance!

Don't underestimate God's placement and purpose—"onto dry land"

God doesn't make any mistakes. Where you are standing (or sitting) right now is no mistake. You are where you are because that is where you are supposed to be.

God's placement is perfect—it is our acceptance of this fact that needs a little work!

Where ever we are placed we must believe there is a purpose behind it—God's purpose (and an eternal purpose).

Let this idea of God's perfect placement sink in—say it out loud—give yourself a pep talk about it. Soon you will see how important it is to accept your current placement in finding personal significance.

First, you have to be at peace with yourself before finding significance in and through your life. The quickest way to peace with yourself is to accept God's perfect placement and purpose in His placement.

Okay now—if God's placement is perfect—then my life is significant. It must be significant!

Thoughts to Ponder

- We shouldn't expect things to go smoothly and then we will never be disappointed. Most of the time—things won't (or don't) go smoothly.

- There are so many times we get it into our heads where the answer is going to come—and thereby miss it when it really does come. The answer can be right before our eyes and never recognize it because we were not thinking of it.

- Making us uncomfortable is God's specialty. It isn't until we are uncomfortable that we are paying attention to God in the first place.

- The most important thing is not how or what—the most important thing is that we learn.

- Let this idea of God's personal placement sink in—say it out loud—give yourself a pep talk about it. Soon will see how important it is to accept your current placement in finding personal significance.

Chapter 17: "3 Days is a Life Time" 3:1-4

¹Now the word of the LORD came to Jonah the second time, saying, ²"Arise, go to Nineveh, that great city, and preach to it the message that I tell you." ³So Jonah arose and went to Nineveh, according to the word of the LORD. Now Nineveh was an exceedingly great city, a three-day journey *in extent.* ⁴And Jonah began to enter the city on the first day's walk. Then he cried out and said, "Yet forty days, and Nineveh shall be overthrown!"

As far as personal significance goes, 3 days is a lifetime!

We can go years of our lives and pretty much hold our own—with nothing really substantially happening. Then—suddenly something happens in one moment that changes everything.

We ought never to take anything for granted. One moment in time can change everything and 3 days can be a lifetime.

The 3 days that Jonah experienced is something that becomes part of ones lifetime memories. Personal significance can be defined for a lifetime from just 3 days, but it is important that we continue to go back to those 3 days as a definition of significance—so we can apply the experience every single day for a lifetime.

God never backs off—if it feels like He has—it isn't Him!

[1]Now the word of the LORD came to Jonah the second time, saying, [2]"Arise, go to Nineveh, that great city, and preach to it the message that I tell you."

God never backs off:

- He never backs off His purpose in our lives.

- He never backs off His direction for our lives.

- He never backs off His intention for us to learn from every situation.

- He never backs off keeping our attention until our own 3 days that lasts a lifetime occurs personally.

- He never backs off reminding us to never back off.

Finding personal significance requires us to realize God is not about backing off—either backing off us or us backing off.

If it seems like it is God who is allowing us to back off—it isn't God at all! Period.

Further—people who do God's work who back off aren't doing God's work!

People have all kinds of excuses for why they don't go all out for God. One of them that often creeps in is the idea that it is all in God's hands now so I can back off....

WRONG!

Everything should be in God's hands—I should surrender it so it is—but it doesn't mean I can back off.

The way personal significance works is: I surrender something to God and then also go all out—not backing off—never backing off—no excuses for ever backing off—and then (and only then) finding personal significance defines my life!

> ## The way you can tell if someone is doing God's work or not is—are they going all out or not?

The purpose of one person's life might exist inside of 3 days of obedience.

³So Jonah arose and went to Nineveh, according to the word of the LORD. Now Nineveh was an exceedingly great city, a three-day journey *in extent.*

In many circles this might be called your "fifteen minutes of fame." Yet—this is much different. These are the 3 days out of all the days of your life by which you will be defined.

Often you can wait your whole life for the 3 days that will define your significance for your entire life. The key is: BE READY WHEN IT COMES!

- Don't expect every day to feel significant—be significant.

- If you haven't experienced any personal significance—position and posture yourself for your 3 days. The days are coming—be sure of it—anticipate and believe your 3 days are just ahead.

- Train yourself to prepare for personal significance—let the training of it be significant in itself.

Seize the moment of mission with everything you've got—it might be all you ever really do!

[4]And Jonah began to enter the city on the first day's walk. Then he cried out and said, "Yet forty days, and Nineveh shall be overthrown!"

When your 3 days of mission do arrive—you probably won't realize <u>this is it</u>. You will probably be thinking it should (or could) last a lot longer. But it doesn't—make the most of what you get.

In the course of your life you will have 3 days of personal significance:

It won't seem that it lasts long enough, but it will be enough for your life time!

<u>Thoughts to Ponder</u>

- We can go years of our lives and pretty much hold our own—with nothing really substantial happening. Then—suddenly something happens in one moment that changes everything.

- Finding personal significance requires us to realize God is not about backing off—backing off us or us backing off the situation (whatever it is we are intending to back off of).

- The way personal significance works is: I surrender something to God and then also go all out—not backing off—never backing off—no excuses for ever backing off—and then (and only then) will I find the personal significance that defines my life!

- When your 3 days do arrive—you probably won't realize that this is the time you have always waited for. Make the most of those 3 days of mission.

Chapter 18: "Right Time—Right Place—Right Person" 3:3-9

[5]So the people of Nineveh believed God, proclaimed a fast, and put on sackcloth, from the greatest to the least of them. [6]Then word came to the king of Nineveh; and he arose from his throne and laid aside his robe, covered *himself* with sackcloth and sat in ashes. [7]And he caused *it* to be proclaimed and published throughout Nineveh by the decree of the king and his nobles, saying—Let neither man nor beast, herd nor flock, taste anything; do not let them eat, or drink water. [8]But let man and beast be covered with sackcloth, and cry mightily to God; yes, let every one turn from his evil way and from the violence that is in his hands. [9]Who can tell *if* God will turn and relent, and turn away from His fierce anger, so that we may not perish?

When Jonah got down to business he made a huge impact on his world. He did something with eternal (and personal) significance.

This was the moment Jonah could always go back to in his thinking when questioning his personal significance.

But—the right time, right place doesn't always happen when we want it to happen. It sometimes happens when we least expect it or when we think it couldn't happen. There are three basic requirements for the moment of significance.

Right Time—Timing is Everything

Everything in life is about the timing. The greatest circumstances can happen, but if it is at the wrong time, the great things carry no significance at all.

On the other hand—little or nothing can happen—but if it is at the right time—it becomes hugely significant in your life. Whether or not you find personal significance through it is up to you—but don't under estimate the little things done at the right time!

The only limitation we have in this regard to the right time and right circumstances is self-induced. We often over estimate an event and under estimate the right time. If we could do just the opposite, we would realize that the most important thing I can do is wait for the right moment.

Waiting for the right moment rather than creating the right event changes the whole possibility in finding personal significance. The waiting itself creates personal significance.

The waiting itself creates personal significance!

Right Place—God's Placement is Part of God's Will

Being at the right place AND the right time? We all operate in the dark.

The only way to make sense of it is to pull the two apart—the right time is one thing and the right place is another.

What can I do about the right place? I have to believe there is a power greater than myself at work in my life (God). In this belief system, the "right place" issues have to fall away as God "orders" our steps.

The right place has to be in the category of God's will. God's placement for me (the right place idea) is right where it should be—hence—I will always be at the right place (at the right time). Further—I may not feel anything significant happening in or through my life at this moment—but I am waiting for the right time because I know I am in the right place (I am living by submitting myself to God's will).

Young people begin to feel the need for God's will when they graduate and don't know what they are supposed to do with their lives. The best way to know God's will is to live according to His Word—and then you will be in the center of His will all the time!

Right Person—Willing Submission

Jonah's life is a perfect example of the wrestling match we all have with submission of our own will.

God specifically gave Jonah a task—clear and simple—but he ran from submitting to God's direction.

Personal significance is never possible until we willingly submit to God's plan, direction, and will for our lives. Until this is done, all you have is the stroking of your ego—but not real significance.

As long as you run from submission you will always be thrown off the ship you jumped on to run away. You can't always count on God sending the fish to swallow you until you come to your senses.

The key is to learn to submit to God early in your life and enjoy personal significance through out your life.

The opposite is also true—do your own thing and spend your life having really having an impact. It is true you could have some really good moments and maybe even a happy life—but you will never find personal significance until you submit your will to God's will!

Thoughts to Ponder

- When Jonah got down to business he made a huge impact on his world—he did something with eternal (and personal) significance.

- Everything in life is about the timing. The greatest things can happen but if it is at the wrong time—the great things carry no significance at all.

- The right place has to be in the category of God's will. God's placement for me (the right place idea) is what it should be—hence—I will always be at the right place (at the right time).

- Personal significance is never possible until we willingly submit to God's plan, direction, and will for our lives. Until this is done all you have is the stroking of your ego—but not real significance.

Chapter 19:
"Turning—Changing—
Molding—Making" 3:10

[10]Then God saw their works, that they turned from their evil way; and God relented from the disaster that He had said He would bring upon them, and He did not do it.

Nothing in life is "inevitable." Everything can change—anything can change!

God's intention was to wipe out Ninevah. But to make sure they had an ample opportunity to turn from their evil ways, He sent Jonah in to proclaim to them their options.

They followed God's message—and He changed their destiny.

Can we change our destiny? At any time you want. Can we change the course of events? More often than you could imagine.

What do we have to do? Just follow the God's Biblical model for turning any situation or person around.

Just follow God's Biblical model and anything can change!

TURN

1st We Turn From Sin

Repentance is the theological word for it—but whatever you call it—it means to turn from your sin.

The importance of this ideal is that it cuts you off from the danger and damage of your previous actions and attitude.

- Repentance creates the tone that you are not intending to continue on your previous course.

- It burns the bridges of unbecoming habits that once controlled you.

- Repentance regards the future as more powerful of an influence upon you than the past.

- It helps to define your direction in a concise and definite way.

- Repentance leaves the way clear for a life of peace not confusion.

We all need a fresh start from time to time. Finding personal significance can seize this dramatic moment of turning from your sin to experience freedom that comes from turning away from those things that negatively influenced and controlled your life.

151

CHANGE

2nd We Change the Condition of Our Hearts

There is only one thing that needs to change—the heart.

If the heart changes then everything else will change!

The idea of the heart is the idea of the inner life—the deepest part of all of us. The condition of change—for it to be true change—has to go deep within the inner life.

The only thing necessary for this transformation to happen is the willingness of a person to have a change in their heart. It isn't about education or equipping—it is simply a decision.

The decision for a heart change happens in an instant. The changing of the heart actually takes place over time as a person faces similar circumstances as before, but this time the person faces them with a new and clean heart. It is at this level that you will see the heart change working in life.

> ## The only thing that ever needs to change is the heart.

MAKE

3rd We Yield (Turn Over) Our Lives to God

Sound tough? How about this: Is your life really working out for you?

Try turning over your life completely to God. Try it this way:

In one powerful moment tell God in your own words that you are turning over your life to Him—from this moment on.

- From this moment on everything that happens to you will be accepted as God's will for you.

- From this moment on you will react to everything as if God personally put everything together for you.

- From this moment on, whenever I doubt the above two things I will go back to that one moment that I did (and know I did)—turn everything over to God.

When ever I am facing something beyond me, I will close my eyes and visually see myself holding the problem in my hands and turning it over to God. I will do this same thing again and again (and again) until I fully get it into my life.

MOLD

4th We Are Shaped into God's Design Through the Circumstances and Situations of Our Lives

This is where the idea of finding personal significance meets together with yielding our lives to God: We are shaped up by God through our circumstances. Our lives become the exercise room for personal growth (and personal significance).

Life is not a test—it is a learning process. God's design for each of us doesn't come instantaneously, but over the course of time through circumstances and situations.

The tougher the circumstance, the greater our potential for advancement in growth—and the more profound the opportunity we have in personal significance.

Yielding our lives to God is not just a mental attitude adjustment—it is a truth—a fundamental principle in the development of our lives.

We are each under God's magnifying glass. He is shaping us, changing us, and developing us. None of us is perfect—we never will be—but we will be equipped and developed to our fullest potential if we yield to God and let it happen!

Thoughts to Ponder

- Nothing in life is "inevitable." Everything can change—anything can change!

- Can we change our destiny? At any time you want. Can we change the course of events? More often than you could imagine.

- We all need a fresh start from time to time. Finding personal significance can seize the dramatic moment of turning from your sin to experience the freedom that comes from turning away from something that negatively influenced (and controlled) your life.

- The decision for a heart change happens in an instant, but the changing of the heart actually takes place over time.

- In one powerful moment, tell God in your own words that you are turning over your life to Him.

- Yielding to God is more than a mental attitude adjustment—it is a truth—a fundamental principle in the development of our lives.

Chapter 20:   "Depression and Other Mental Illnesses" 4:1-3

¹But it displeased Jonah exceedingly and he became angry. ²So he prayed to the LORD, and said, "Ah, LORD, was not this what I said when I was still in my country? Therefore I fled previously to Tarshish; for I know that You *are* a gracious and merciful God, slow to anger and abundant in loving kindness, One who relents from doing harm. ³Therefore now, O LORD, please take my life from me, for *it is* better for me to die than to live!"

In this passage, we see the down side to Jonah's emotions, and his struggle with mental stability. The impact of Jonah's honesty while in this mental state is huge!

Throughout the years, mental health has often been seen as a joke or source of laughter. We misunderstand issues like depression—to the point where we believe that if a person were just a little stronger the depression would disappear.

No one wants to be considered crazy—so many people who need mental help never get it because of the stigma associated with the admission of problems like depression.

Jonah was depressed. He was moody—angry—and irrational. What is our typical response to people like him? We ignore them, chase them off, or trap them.

Jonah needed help. He didn't need to be judged or treated like he was crazy. His three days in Ninevah provided him personal significance, but it was on the throes of being taken away because of mental illness.

Mental illness will do exactly that—rob a person of every ounce of self worth. Additionally, the stigma associated with mental illness creates a climate for a person to run away or actually go crazy—all this when all they needed was some help.

Mental illness is no different from physical illness when it comes to a need for treatment. It is time we start teaching people this truth.

The next step would be to help people who are experiencing different forms of personal significance. These people striving for significance are definitely a target for experiencing an imbalance of body chemistry. Any time a person has to put a lot out there—exert energy—experience emotional trauma—or mental concentration—there is always the potential of an emotional/mental imbalance to occur.

We shouldn't be caught off guard by emotional or mental imbalance or behavior. We should be prepared to handle and help guide those people who are experiencing it.

Even in God's work you can become disoriented.

Some people think that you can't become distracted or disoriented in God's work. Jonah's three days in Ninevah is a good example of it.

You would have thought Jonah would have been happy, not angry about God changing His mind and not destroying Ninevah after the people repented. This kind of unpredictable attitude and behavior is typical in those who have gone through an intense period of exertion.

Jonah walked through Ninevah preaching repentance. Would that have been easy to do? It wouldn't have been easy for anyone to do. The amount of emotional energy required for this task put Jonah's body chemistry in an imbalance.

Jonah became disoriented first, and then he became angry. God tried to help him, but Jonah was too disoriented to be helped.

Somewhere in the course of the unraveling, finding personal significance didn't mean anything to Jonah. Mental health issues totally consumed any remnant of personal significance. We should watch out for people putting too much energy into something. We should help out others during their time frame of exertion—or we will be dealing with the depression later.

It is important to monitor yourself well to be honest with how you feel.

There are two parts to monitoring:

1. **Monitor how you feel. Don't play games with how you feel before, during and after something that requires all you have got to give. The key is to brace for those times of intensity. The most important thing is to take breaks—release the pressure—let off the steam. Otherwise you will be setting your body chemistry off balance and askew.**

2. **Honesty with yourself. It doesn't help to monitor yourself if you aren't being honest about how you feel. If you aren't honest about how you feel, you aren't able to get any help because you won't admit you need help. Honesty was Jonah's problem from the very start.**

Monitoring and honesty might not change the entire course of events—but it will help you get a handle on the problem. Handling the problem sooner than later (where clinical depression leaves a person helpless) is the key to success in preventing mental illness. Monitoring and honesty are also the keys to maintaining a sense of personal significance even if emotional/mental illness rattles your cage just a little bit!

Don't let a body chemistry problem become a mental illness—that is why God becomes involved.

You can stop a potential problem in its tracks if you know what you are looking for.

What are you looking for?

- The person who doesn't let anything get in his/her way once they get started.

- The person who resists at first but eventually gives it their all.

- The person who doesn't take breaks or won't listen to anyone during the process of the work.

- The person who is required to put himself really out there regardless of potential embarrassment or rejection.

If you know these people or observe these kinds of behaviors, you need to create procedures or guidelines of involvement. Include the requirement of breaks—consultations—fact finding—review sessions.

Do anything you can to help take the edge off of others.

The only way to get help is to first help yourself by applying the truth you know to your own life.

You can't help a person who doesn't want to be helped. In the same way, you can't reach a person who doesn't want to be reached. This is what makes it so difficult to reach out to someone with a mental illness. They will often seem unreachable because they are emotionally or mentally unstable.

Unless a person lets you, you can't help them—but then—no one said you can fix everything. We do our best and leave it to God.

The tricky part about helping someone who is depressed is exactly this problem—some may not want help or acknowledge the need for help. When this happens, you have to let it go and move on.

If you are the person who is struggling with an imbalance, instability, and/or depression remember that help is available. People want to help you—even if you don't realize it—BUT YOU HAVE TO LET THEM HELP YOU!

The best help you can ever find is when you swallow your pride, drop your defenses, and let others help you heal.

Thoughts to Ponder

- Jonah was depressed. He was moody—angry—and irrational. What is our typical response to people like him? We ignore them, chase them off, or trap them.

- Mental illness is no different from physical illness when it comes to a need for treatment. It is time we start teaching people this truth.

- You would have thought Jonah would have been happy, not angry about God changing His mind and not destroying Ninevah after they repented. This kind of unpredictable attitude and behavior is typical in those who have gone through an intense period of exertion.

- Monitoring and honesty might not change the entire course of events—but it will help you get the handle on the problem.

- If you know people or observe mental illness you need to create procedures or guidelines of involvement.

- Unless a person lets you, you can't help them. We do our best and leave it to God.

Chapter 21: "Manage Your Emotions—Getting Worked Up" 4:4

⁴**Then the LORD said, "*Is it* right for you to be angry?"**

God asks Jonah a question that cuts right through it all—is it right for you to get yourself so worked up?

This question has a larger application than just to Jonah at that moment—it is a universal question to all of us when it starts to happen to us.

Is it right for you to get yourself all worked up?

This question is obviously rhetorical. However, for the people who try to answer the question, their character is revealed. Jonah's response to God made Jonah look like a spoiled brat.

When asked the question, that in itself should be enough to get our attention. Do you have the right to get yourself all worked up? No—of course not—

Getting worked up only makes matters worse. Getting worked up never solves anything!

1. We never have the right to be worked up.

Personal defensiveness goes right along with getting worked up. A person who is worked up or getting worked up is going to be highly defensive about it. Personal defensiveness will always include justification and blame.

What we must understand about getting worked up is—there is nothing that will happen while being worked up that will help gain personal significance.

Further—each of us has the power within ourselves to calm ourselves back down. Calming down is a decision. Each person decides his/her own course of action and reaction in this arena.

It would be to your advantage when facing situations that get you worked up, to remind yourself: "I have no right to get worked up!"

"I have no right to get worked up—it doesn't do me, those around me, or the situation any good!"

164

2. Getting worked up is always dangerous for yourself and others.

Getting worked up is dangerous in many ways, including the realm of the potential for violence:

- Getting worked up is dangerous to your reputation. If people are scared of you they won't approach you—they will even speak negatively about you behind your back.

- Getting worked up is dangerous to your career. It is a stigma that will follow you. If you are successful the stigma will stay at bay—but if not, getting worked up will bite you at the first (and every time after that) opportunity.

- Getting worked up is dangerous to your mental health. If people avoid you the feeling of rejection will harm your emotional/mental stability.

- Getting worked up is dangerous to your relationships. If people feel like they have to handle you with "kid gloves" your relationships will never develop depth.

3. Getting worked up is never positive.

There is absolutely nothing positive about getting worked up. Both getting worked up and the consequences of getting worked up are not positive.

Think of the negative affects of getting worked up:

- People in general will avoid me—which at first might sound positive—but we all need people in many ways we don't acknowledge. If people consistently avoid me, the consequences won't be positive.

- People won't trust me. If people think I can get worked up quickly—it will seem to them that I am a bully. When people think you bully them—or there is a possibility that you will bully them—they won't trust you.

- The more I get worked up—the more I will get worked up. Getting worked up not only does negative things to relationships but to one's health as well. Getting worked up will change your body chemistry. It can create a huge imbalance and subsequently harmful health issues.

It may not be possible to "flip a switch" and change (if you are known to get yourself worked up)—but let these ideas sink in a little at a time.

4. Getting worked up will provide you with tons of extra work.

Anyone who gets worked up has two time consuming aspects to deal with: 1) the energy used in getting worked up itself. 2) The work required to right the wrongs you did while you were worked up.

Getting worked up is a waste of time. Do you really have the time for the extra work? Generally speaking when you are getting worked up, your concentration and application are at lower levels. You just can't be very productive when you get worked up.

The aftermath of getting worked up is the real time zapper. Almost everyone who gets himself worked up has a period of time after things get calmed down that require things get smoothed over.

Hopefully a person who gets worked up will feel guilty and apologize to those around him. Do you really enjoy apologizing? If not, this provides the motivation to quit getting worked up. If you enjoy apologizing (messing up and apologizing) you actually are displaying addictive behavior (not the subject of this book).

If there is no guilt, the self-justified person creates a huge scenario that includes long periods of discussions—negotiations—and further periods of getting worked up (repetition of this cycle).

5. Getting worked up is always unnecessary, time consuming, energy zapping, and silly.

Getting worked up accomplishes nothing at all—that is why it is unnecessary. If something doesn't accomplish anything—we should consider it unnecessary in our lives.

Getting worked up robs you of your time. You can always be doing something beneficial during the time frame it takes you to get worked up. Multi-task individuals are especially prone to waste their time when they get worked up. Where they usually would be productive at many levels—everything stops dead while they get themselves under control.

Getting worked up zaps your energy. Not only does it affect the person who gets worked up but also those around the person who gets worked up. People get exhausted dealing with the person who is worked up and the person worked up gets exhausted. (This would be another reason why getting worked up is unnecessary).

Furthermore—getting worked up is just plain silly. The things we get worked up about are usually the silliest of silly things. The stories people tell after the fact about what they got worked up about and why is something that should be analyzed carefully because silliness is always involved. We should learn this lesson quickly—getting worked up is silly!

6. Develop your own template and apply it when you feel you are getting worked up.

Each person is different--and different things "push your buttons" to get you worked up.

Each person should determine what the triggers are that would cause you to get worked up. AFTER THAT—AVOID THE TRIGGERS!

Further—each person should have a contingency in place once a trigger is set off. It is going to happen (not if but when). A person who gets worked up is not going to be able to change over night.

The contingency idea is a kind of "template" to deal with getting worked up.

The following is a basic template—adjust it—change it—but make it your own.

A) Every day I will start the day by talking to myself about staying calm and balanced. "I won't get myself worked up today."

B) If a trigger gets set I will be immediately conscious of my need to talk myself down—"I don't need to get worked up. I'm not going to get worked up."

C) I will have people around me whom I trust completely and who know me. I will trust them to point out to me my danger zones, soft spots and triggers. When they point them out I won't get myself worked up with them—but accept their help.

D) I will put something into place that will remind me to get myself back together and collect my wits once again. (It could be a rubber band around your wrist that you snap when you feel yourself becoming worked up).

E) I will create positive outlets for my energy when I feel myself getting worked up. (I will work out; read; go to a movie; or pray).

F) I will make my connection with God through prayer my most important meeting of the day.

G) Whenever I feel myself getting worked up it will be a reminder to me that my relationship with God is not as focused or centered as it should be.

What does all of this have to do with finding personal significance? If you can't keep yourself from getting worked up—if you can't manage your emotions—you will never find personal significance. It will be too elusive to you—and even if it does become present in your life you wouldn't recognize it because of how self-absorbed you are (through always getting worked up).

Thoughts to Ponder

- We must understand there is nothing that will happen while being worked up that will help me gain personal significance.

- Getting worked up is dangerous to your relationships. If people feel like they have to handle you with "kid gloves" your relationships will never be very deep.

- The more I get worked up—the more I will get worked up. Getting worked up not only affects relationships negatively, but one's health as well. Getting worked up will change your body chemistry. It can create an imbalance and subsequently harmful health issues.

- Anyone who gets worked up has two time consuming things to deal with: 1) Getting worked up itself, and 2) The work required to right the wrongs you did while you were worked up.

- Getting worked up zaps your energy. Not only does it affect the person who gets worked up but also those around the person who gets worked up.

Chapter 22: "Manage Your Emotions—Turning Your Pain into Potential" 4:5-11

[5]So Jonah went out of the city and sat on the east side of the city. There he made himself a shelter and sat under it in the shade, till he might see what would become of the city. [6]And the LORD God prepared a plant and made it come up over Jonah, that it might be shade for his head to deliver him from his misery. So Jonah was very grateful for the plant. [7]But as morning dawned the next day God prepared a worm, and it *so* damaged the plant that it withered. [8]And it happened, when the sun arose, that God prepared a vehement east wind; and the sun beat on Jonah's head, so that he grew faint. Then he wished death for himself, and said, "*It is* better for me to die than to live."

[9]Then God said to Jonah, "*Is it* right for you to be angry about the plant?"

And he said, "*It is* right for me to be angry, even to death!"

[10]But the LORD said, "You have had pity on the plant for which you have not labored, nor made it grow, which came up in a night and perished in a night. [11]And should I not pity Nineveh, that great city, in which are more than one hundred and twenty thousand persons who cannot discern between their right hand and their left—and much livestock?"

Managing emotions requires not getting yourself worked up and harnessing your pain. Getting control and managing your own pain releases your potential. It is as easy as applying some simple steps.

Limit the time you allow yourself to just sit around—it causes too much negative personalized reflection!

[5]So Jonah went out of the city and sat on the east side of the city.

Reflection is one thing—ruminating on something is completely different—and very dangerous.

When Jonah went out of the city to watch what was happening it gave him a lot of time to think about things. His mind did the natural thing we all do—create negative scenarios.

This always happens when we take too much time just sitting around. Staying active creates productivity, creativity, and strength—Sitting around makes you soft, stoic, and stuffy.

Thinking about your pain is more painful—contemplating your hurt makes you more sensitive—analyzing your problems creates spin off problems.

After a while it all becomes about me—which endows more pain than the beginning. When you are only thinking about you it is you're only comparable. Everything becomes about you and your pain.

When you clear your head by occupying your mind with other thoughts and life with other activities—you will begin to harness your pain and manage your emotions.

Exercise caution when doing something just for yourself—it increases the potential for making things about you and hence bring on more pain.

"There he made himself a shelter and sat under it in the shade"

Emotional reactions create selfish behaviors. These behaviors do nothing to bring healing to the pain. It enhances the self pity and intensifies the self absorption.

When people are in pain (or emotionally out of balance) they will do things because they feel self-empowered to "do something extra for myself." As normal as it feels it is a dangerous thing to do.

When you are in pain you don't need to cuddle yourself, you need to harness it!

When you are in pain don't feel sorry for yourself—harness it!

174

Never be just an observer—it takes away your stake in the game and makes you more selfish, critical, scrutinizing and nit picky.

"Till he might see what would become of the city."

People who just sit back and watch usually end up being the biggest critic of all—because they have no stake in the game or ownership of what is going on.

Unless you have ownership or at least a stake in a situation you will always be more critical. The best example of this is how critical people can be of something unless their own loved ones are involved and then their outlook changes completely.

Sitting back and watching doesn't help with managing emotions/harnessing pain. It actually causes greater pain because nothing other people do will ever be good enough if you don't have a stake in the game.

> **If you catch yourself being critical it is because you don't have a large enough stake in the game—so step up!**

Always be thankful—even for the smallest blessing.

[6]And the LORD God prepared a plant and made it come up over Jonah, that it might be shade for his head to deliver him from his misery. So Jonah was very grateful for the plant.

Most importantly restore your perspective to any situation. Restoring your perspective is essential.

Regardless of your situation—what you are facing—or the pain you have/are enduring—thankfulness helps to harness it properly.

"Jonah was grateful for the plant"—in this Jonah was a positive example for us. He isn't able to keep hold of his joy at this level—but at least for a short amount of time we can see how it all works together.

Start with the smallest thing—be thankful for it. It will at least help you get your mind off yourself or your pain for a little while—and a little while is often enough time to start seeing things change for you.

It shouldn't even start with a question: "What am I thankful for?" It should be a commitment to a statement that I make every day:

What is it I am thankful for?

Hold on to everything lightly—it is all just temporary—don't take anything for granted.

> ⁷But as morning dawned the next day God prepared a worm, and it *so* damaged the plant that it withered. ⁸And it happened, when the sun arose, that God prepared a vehement east wind; and the sun beat on Jonah's head, so that he grew faint. Then he wished death for himself, and said, "*It is* better for me to die than to live."

Enjoy the moment you are in right now—don't take anything for granted. If you do—you are in for a huge disappointment. The more things you take for granted the larger your potential is to be disappointed.

Holding on to things lightly is that continual reminder that nothing in life is permanent. Jonah had a little shade for a little while but thought it was his to possess, control and own. God sent the worm to eat the vine giving the shade to prove some things to Jonah and to us—that nothing in life is permanent.

If we hold tightly (rather than lightly) to things we will develop the emotional problems associated with not being unable to control the things we want to control. People who have to fix things fall into this category. Know yourself enough to realize where you are coming from in regard to this.

When you get yourself focused on yourself you become unreasonable quickly.

> Then God said to Jonah, "*Is it* right for you to be angry about the plant?" And he said, "*It is* right for me to be angry, even to death!"

It is a fact that when you are focused on YOU—you become unreasonable—and very quickly at that.

The first matter is to accept this fact. When I am centered on me I am unreasonable—now we can work to solve the problem:

- If I accept the fact that when I am focused on me I am unreasonable—I don't have to deal with how logical I am sounding but if I am focused on me or not.

- A huge amount of honesty is required—but the honesty is easier than the arguments created by a person who is focused upon self.

- Hence—I never have to deal with my arguments until I first deal with my focus.

Pain that comes from not managing one's emotions is a sure way to focus on you. Pain has a way of setting up a person's world around self because of the way it robs a person of his/her entire focus.

Yield to God and follow the grand design of the big picture!

There is both a grand design and a big picture and you can have them both if you yield yourself to God.

Yielding to God is what managing your emotions all is about because resisting God is what pain is all about. Jonah was a good example of a person who didn't yield to God and was in all kinds of pain.

The ability to turn your pain into something good is all up to you! Even the pain has an unlimited potential to help you grow if you yield your life—your attitude and actions—to God completely.

The choice is yours: Sit up on a hill and feel sorry for yourself for no reason (multiplying your pain) or yield yourself to God—take on a thankful spirit and release your unlimited potential.

> **Which do you chose:**
> **A yielded, thankful life with an unlimited potential or an unstable emotional life filled with pain?**
> **IT IS ALL UP TO YOU!**

Thoughts to Ponder

- Thinking about your pain is more painful—contemplating your hurt makes you more sensitive—analyzing your problems creates spin off problems.

- Start with the smallest thing—be thankful for it. It will at least help you get your mind off yourself or your pain for a little while—and a little while is often enough time to start seeing things change for you.

- Enjoy the moment you are in right now—don't take anything for granted. If you do—you are in for a huge disappointment. The more things you take for granted the larger your potential is to be disappointed.

- Pain that comes from not managing one's emotions is a sure way to focus on you. Pain has a way of setting up a person's world around self because of the way it robs a person of his or her entire focus.

- Yielding to God is what managing your emotions all is about because resisting God is what pain is all about. Jonah was a good example of a person who didn't yield to God and was in all kinds of pain.

CONCLUDING THOUGHTS

Finding personal significance is an on going endeavor. It isn't something you should ever feel like is finished because the basic essence of finding personal significance is never finished—a life completely centered upon God.

Jonah was a good example...a bad example...up and down...good decision and bad decision but above all—Jonah was the right example to use for this study. There are many examples of real living and real emotion in this short story.

Finding personal significance needs to be the same as Jonah—a real thing—and real people.

The bumps along the road of life can sometimes be difficult but we can always find personal significance no matter what it is we face.

The desire you have had by taking this journey together shows something significant—that is—you are already finding personal significance!